D0349668

PRAISE FOR
HOSPITALITY FROM THE HEART

"Ingenious and spot-on! The principles of *Hospitality from the Heart* will evoke emotional memories of all that you believe about business, but may have forgotten through everyday stresses. The authors clearly illustrate the differences between the highly successful and the struggling. These principles do not need to be *learned* so much as *recognized, remembered,* and *lived.*"

LEN GHILANI, FOUNDER AND CEO OF GHILANI GROUP, INC.

"I loved this book! The principles of *Hospitality from the Heart* are simple and at the same time incredibly profound. This book is a road map for every business person to help build a culture that inspires passionate engagement and generates outstanding high-performance bottom-line results. A fabulous and fun read, and just as important, awesome learning!"

CHRISTOPHER M. O'DONNELL, DIRECTOR, PRESIDENT AND COO, FAMOUS DAVE'S OF AMERICA

"*Hospitality from the Heart* is both validating and eye-opening. This book helps readers to connect the dots between their hearts and the hearts and minds of their guests. If you want to create the single most sustainable differentiator between you and your competition, read this book, don't put it down until you're done, then read it again."

CHUCK PATON, GENERAL MANAGER, LARSMONT COTTAGES ON LAKE SUPERIOR

"If you want to drive top-line revenues and move your team members from satisfying customers to loyal guests, then *Hospitality from the Heart* is a must read for general managers and department heads. My Executive Committee and I spent two amazing days in the Leadership from the Heart training workshop, and we will be using these strategies into 2013 and beyond. This book captures the guiding principles from the two days and then provides you with a step-by-step implementation plan."

JOHN E. LUKE, GENERAL MANAGER, HILTON–MINNEAPOLIS

"*Hospitality from the Heart* will make you want to be a better person. It will challenge you by self-examination. It's a fantastic combination of humor and honesty. If you have been struggling to master the successful combination of employee engagement, guest loyalty, and service beyond words, then this book is the key to professional success while achieving personal satisfaction! A must read for everyone!"

SARA LEBENS, AREA HUMAN RESOURCES DIRECTOR, HYATT HOTELS CORPORATION

"A captivating story that reminds the reader that the small things matter! An essential tool in the toolkit for all service businesses with a critical reminder: lead from your HEART. I wholeheartedly support this book and its reminders about what is important."

JACKIE KANE OTTOSON, VICE PRESIDENT OF HR, TRAINING, AND COMMUNICATION, FAMOUS DAVE'S OF AMERICA

"What a delight! *Hospitality from the Heart* is a treasure trove of ideas and practices. This book is a source of truly uncommon wisdom. I know I will draw heavily on it in my own personal and professional journey."

TOM FELTENSTEIN, PRESIDENT AND CEO, POWER MARKETING ACADEMY

"We have met few individuals who truly walk their talk, who live their life the way they teach the rest of the world to live it. Brandon is one of those rare individuals. The HEART concept is one that inspires a positive environment where the employees AND customers enjoy being. His ongoing, personal dedication to bringing positive energy to a frequently negative, gloomy society is an inspiration to all who are fortunate enough to read this book or attend an event."

TIM REYNOLDS, MD, CEO AND PAMELA REYNOLDS, COO; OWNERS OF HEALTHCARE EXPRESS URGENT CARE CENTERS

"Hospitality from the Heart tells what it takes to truly be great in the hospitality industry. This book is an excellent read for young hospitality professionals who are trying to understand the importance of people and guests."

BRIAN BERGQUIST, PHD, PROFESSOR, SCHOOL OF HOSPITALITY, UNIVERSITY OF WISCONSIN—STOUT

"Hospitality from the Heart shares a vision that drives you to leverage your strengths, develop your skills, explore your growth opportunities, and serve from the heart. Brandon and Katherine are leading others to serve with the heart of inclusive and engaged leaders— join them on this journey to success!"

ANGELA LAGOS, SENIOR MANAGER DIVERSITY & INCLUSION, UNIVERSAL PARKS & RESORTS

HOSPITALITY
FROM THE
HEART

*Energy is
Everything!*

*May this Story & the
HEART principles serve you on
your journey to being Extraordinary!

With St Energy —*

HOSPITALITY
FROM THE
HEART

Engage Your Employees,
Deliver Extraordinary Service,
and Create Loyal Guests

BRANDON W. JOHNSON
AND KATHERINE FOLEY RODEN

BEAVER'S
POND
PRESS

HOSPITALITY FROM THE HEART © copyright 2013 by
Brandon W. Johnson and Katherine Foley Roden.
All rights reserved. No part of this book may be reproduced in any
form whatsoever, by photography or xerography or by any other means,
by broadcast or transmission, by translation into any kind of language,
nor by recording electronically or otherwise, without permission in
writing from the author, except by a reviewer, who may quote brief
passages in critical articles or reviews.

ISBN 13: 978-1-59298-579-1

Library of Congress Catalog Number: 2012922878

Printed in the United States of America

First Printing: 2013

17 16 15 14 13   5 4 3 2 1

Cover and interior design by James Monroe Design, LLC.

Beaver's Pond Press, Inc.
7108 Ohms Lane
Edina, MN 55439–2129
(952) 829-8818
www.BeaversPondPress.com

BEAVER'S
POND
PRESS

To order, visit www.BeaversPondBooks.com
or call (800) 901-3480. Reseller discounts available.

For my parents, Jim and Cindy, for the love, encouragement, and support while raising me to be the man, father, and husband that I am today. For Emma and Zachary, for being my teachers in how to live from my heart and bring positive energy to this world. And for my beautiful and wonderful wife, Katie, who has shown me that love, commitment, and heart have no boundaries.

—BWJ

For my parents, Bill and Jane, my greatest teachers of true hospitality—for raising me to have heart. And for Roger— for showing me just how great a heart can be.

—KFR

And for all of the friends, mentors, coaches, and colleagues whose guidance, love, and support have made this book possible. We thank you for the consistent urging and encouragement to share our message with the world.
You live in this book—as you do in our hearts.

—BWJ and KFR

CONTENTS

PART I
JIM'S STORY

PART II
YOUR STORY

INTRODUCTION

In today's world, people are not starving for information. In fact, we are overwhelmed with information; we're drowning in it. What we are starving for is connection. Yes, we have Facebook and Twitter, but we spend more time in solitary activities than we have at any other time in the history of mankind. This explosion of time spent staring at screens—whether of the television, computer, or smartphone variety—has, in essentially one generation, pillaged both the time and quality of the connections we make with one another. One 2010 survey reported that more than 44 million people in the United States suffer from loneliness and a longing to connect with others. Surprisingly, working people in their forties and fifties from all walks of life reported feeling lonely the most.

In any industry, but certainly in the hospitality industry, those are your customers, your guests. They are also your employees, your peers, and, most likely, you. So how can you conduct the business of your business—whatever that may be—in a way that counteracts this troubling trend? How can you create an environment that forges and nurtures meaningful connections between your business and your customers, between your leadership team and your employees, and among your employees themselves? And is creating these connections really important to the bottom line? Can it improve sales and profits, make your business flourish? Yes, it can. People invest their time and money in businesses and services that make them feel seen, cared for, and connected—especially when it comes to those businesses and services in the hospitality industry.

That's what this book is about.

In part I, you'll meet Jim Watts, a fictional hospitality executive who has literally and figuratively lost his way. He's been successful in his rise up the ladder, yet he's unhappy and fighting a battle using the wrong weapon. You cannot win the hearts of others, whether your employees or guests, using only your head. His fictional journey is based on the real-life struggles we have encountered both as individuals and with our clients over the past twenty years. You may ask, "Is it really so important to win my guests' hearts?" Well, according to a 2009 Service Management Group study of 100 million people, loyal customers drive top-line growth. When you are able to shift a "satisfied" guest to a "highly satisfied" guest, they are twice as likely to return than those who were simply "satisfied." That's customer loyalty. And, by the way, the same study showed loyal guests spend more, complain less, and are less price sensitive. And they are also three times more likely to recommend your business to others. That creates top-line growth.

So if you're satisfied with "satisfied"—what we call "good 'nuff"—then keep doing what you're doing. You may do fine. You may make a profit. But if you want to tip the scales in your favor—if you want to build a legacy of service and profitability, of engaged employees who are committed to your organization, and of loyal customers who can't wait to tell their friends about you—then you are ready to learn the principles of Hospitality from the HEART.

Some of Jim's challenges will likely resonate with you because in our decades of experience working in the hospitality industry—Brandon in restaurants and hotels and Katherine in casino resorts—they are challenges we've encountered again and again.

Jim's story also introduces you to the concept of HEART— Humility, Energy x Execution, Awareness, Relationships, and Trust = Teamwork—principles that allow you to engage your employees, deliver extraordinary service, and create loyal guests.

Part II of this book provides you with a step-by-step guide to implement the five principles of HEART in your organization. We'll share real-life examples of the impact each of the principles can have on an organization's culture as well as its bottom line. We'll also provide guiding questions so you can evaluate your performance in those areas. And finally, we'll give you action steps to bring the principles of HEART to life in your organization. HEART-centered companies are not born—they are developed. Creating a *Hospitality from the HEART* culture is actually simple, yet it's hard. In today's world, simple is hard. But it's worth it.

We've seen astounding performance from organizations that have found and followed their HEART. Consider companies such as Google, Zappos, and Whole Foods Market—some of the most profitable companies in the history of business. They all exemplify the HEART-centered culture we'll share with you. They are honored repeatedly by *Fortune* magazine as some of the best companies to work for. When you create an environment where people love to work, you create an environment your guests love, too. We want that level of success for you, which is the reason why we've come together to create this book.

With HEART and in Service to Your Success,

—BRANDON AND KATHERINE
MINNEAPOLIS, MINNESOTA
JANUARY 2013

PART I

JIM'S STORY

THE STORM

It was snowing hard the night Jim and Amanda Watts slid
into the parking lot of the Gottschalk Inn. Jim struggled to
hide his disdain when Amanda looked out at the snow-covered
pines and the rustic wood-and-stone lodge and said, "Oh! It's
just darling! It's kind of fun and romantic—being stranded in
the snow at a quaint little lodge in the woods!" Jim just kept
wishing they'd taken the Land Rover rather than the BMW
from Chicago to Minneapolis for the hospitality conference.
He was also wishing he'd just flown and left Amanda at
home. Now he would be holed up out here, thirty miles from
nowhere, waiting for roads to clear—probably without Wi-Fi
and certainly without a decent bottle of scotch.

He'd already been out of the office most of the week,
wasting valuable time at that unhelpful hotel conference in
Minneapolis. Now getting caught in this storm on the way
home to Chicago meant he was most likely going to miss the

Friday meeting with the board and the investors. That part he wasn't sure he minded so much. He'd been getting a lot of pressure from the board to increase revenue and service, and in a down economy, he just didn't see how he could do it. No one at the conference seemed to impart any real wisdom, either. He couldn't believe he'd spent three and a half days listening to so-called experts drone on about cheaper labor and cheaper cuts of beef. What a waste. No one really seemed to feel the sense of urgency he felt. He was pretty sure his career was on the line.

He felt Amanda just didn't understand him, either. She was always so emotional about things; it drove him nuts. He loved her. At least, he was pretty sure he did. They'd been together long enough—twenty-eight years. Their kids, Jack and Emma, were both grown now and living on their own. Jack had a job in LA doing film editing, and Em was finishing her master's in psychology at NYU. It seemed that ever since the kids moved out, Amanda had been a little lost—as if she didn't know what to do with herself.

All he knew was that at the moment, he didn't see a "quaint little inn" before them. The evergreens heavy with snow that looked so charming to Amanda looked desperate to him—weighed down, somewhat like Jim himself, nearly to the point of breaking. He saw a rather ramshackle little place in Middle-of-Nowhere, Wisconsin. The map said they were near Lake Geneva, theoretically only ninety minutes from Chicago—except now they were in a blinding snowstorm. He just couldn't believe he'd let Amanda talk him into getting so far off the interstate. She'd heard about the Gottschalk Inn from a friend and was sure it was "right off the road." So much for that.

They parked near the main entrance, and as they began to unload their bags, Jim caught the sound of crunching snow behind him. "Hi there!" a man's voice called out. Jim and Amanda turned in surprise to see a tall young man bounding toward them through the snow-covered lot. "Hi! Let me get those for you. You guys just head right in and get warm by the fire. I'm Adam, by the way. Welcome to the Gottschalk Inn."

Jim and Amanda were glad to accept his offer and made their way quickly to the doors as Adam deftly gathered their bags and carried them through the rapidly accumulating snow and into the lobby of the lodge. As they entered and stamped the heavy, wet snow from their shoes, what greeted them was more movie-like than real. The main lodge had a vaulted ceiling with rough-hewn, dark-wood beams. Opposite the main entrance was a massive stone fireplace, complete with a warm, crackling fire. The fireplace was flanked by giant windows. Jim thought they had to be at least fifteen feet tall. There were elk, deer, and caribou heads on the walls, and the furniture was rustic and well worn, but clean and in good repair. Amanda's thoughts lifted with her eyes as she followed the massive arch of the ceiling from one side to the other. She breathed in deeply the earthy aroma of the wood fire combined with the clean smell of furniture polish. She whispered, more to herself than anyone else, "Wow. This is fantastic."

Jim thought to himself, "Oh, great. I'm in that freaky Jack Nicholson movie."

As they stood before the fire and took it all in, Adam appeared from behind the front desk, where he'd apparently gone to remove his coat, hat, and boots. Amanda figured he was probably in his early twenties. He was tall and athletic looking. Not linebacker athletic, though; he was lean like a runner. His nearly black hair was tousled, most likely from the speedy removal of his hat, and though his eyes were dark brown, there was a light to them that reminded her of Jack's.

"That's some storm!" Adam said. "I'm glad you arrived safely. Would you like something hot to drink?" He gestured to a little coffee service set out of the way. "We've got coffee and plenty of hot water for tea or cocoa."

Amanda said, "Tea sounds really good about now," and strolled over to the table. She smiled when she saw the mismatched but pretty porcelain mugs and the big old-fashioned tea chest filled with a wide variety of teas from all over the world. She chose one and poured the hot water. As her tea steeped, she followed the trail of aromatic steam and noticed two hand-painted plaques above the table. The first said:

> *"We can do no great things,*
> *only small things with great love.*
> —MOTHER TERESA."

The second said:

> *"If you want to speak to the heart of a man,*
> *you must speak from your own."*

The second plaque's quote was uncredited. She wrapped her hands around her mug of tea and felt the warmth radiate into her palms. She felt warmer on the inside as well—though she wasn't entirely sure why.

As Amanda fixed her tea, Jim wanted to get down to the business of check-in. He turned to Adam and said, "I hope to God you've got a room available, because we need one for the night, and we don't have reservations."

Adam said, "You've come to the right place. We've had a few cancellations because of the weather. Have you stayed with us before?"

"Uh, *no*," Jim answered, not making any effort to hide his superior tone. "We're not really the rustic types. We're from Chicago."

"Well, welcome. I think you'll really love it here. Lots of folks come here from the city to relax and unplug for a while," Adam replied.

Ironically, that reminded Jim about the Wi-Fi. "Do you have high-speed Internet in the rooms? Or Wi-Fi access?"

"No, here at Gottschalk Inn, we really focus on the basics. We have Internet access on two computers in our business center. Our guest rooms are designed for peace and solitude."

Jim just about snorted. "Peace and solitude, eh? Young man, the way I work, those two words are not in my vocabulary. Is your business center open twenty-four hours?"

For just a moment, Adam's bright eyes flashed a look that seemed an awful lot like compassion. Jim dismissed it, thinking surely Adam could not comprehend the challenges a successful COO of a large hospitality company faced. He looked Adam over—in his jeans and comfortable plaid shirt—and thought he seemed utterly average. *What could this under-achiever possibly see in* me *that warrants pity?* he said to himself.

Adam's response to his question brought him back to the moment. "Yes, the business center is open twenty-four hours. It's just down the main hall a bit on the right—past the lounge, which is open until midnight."

"Lounge, as in *bar*?" Jim smiled for the first time in hours. "Now you're talking my language. Even cheap scotch at this point would be better than no scotch."

"If you enjoy scotch, you'll definitely want to visit with Mike at the bar. He's pretty much an expert," Adam said.

Jim thought, *I doubt anyone out here in the boonies could tell the difference between scotch whisky and Scotch Tape . . . but whatever.*

As Adam proceeded to check them in, Amanda sidled up next to Jim, tea still in hand. She looked over the desk and saw a large textbook titled *Immunology: An Illustrated Outline*. She pointed to it and said, "A little light reading?"

Adam almost apologetically moved the massive book to a shelf below the counter. He said, "No, just a little studying when I'm not needed elsewhere."

She said, "Immunology is hardly a 'little' studying. You must be in medical school."

"I am," he said.

"Where do you go to school?"

"Oh, I go to Pritzker."

Jim, who had been fishing in his briefcase for his wallet and largely ignoring the whole interaction, stopped what he was doing. He looked up at Adam with surprise and curiosity. He said, "Pritzker? As in, the University of Chicago? As in, one of the top medical schools in the country?"

Adam blushed a little and replied, "That's the one. I've always been interested in science and in serving others. I've had a lot of encouragement and support. I feel very lucky to be there."

Jim shook his head and said, "You don't get into Pritzker on luck, son—even I know *that*. What on earth are you doing, working way the heck out here?"

"I really love it here. I worked here all through high school and during my undergraduate summer breaks. The owner lets me come back and help out when I can. It's a pretty special place. It may sound a little silly, but working here keeps me grounded."

Amanda smiled at Adam and said, "Would it be possible for us to stay until Sunday?"

Adam met her eyes and smiled back. "I think we can do that. Just give me a moment to double-check," he replied.

Jim looked at Amanda as if she'd suddenly sprouted green hair. He just about exploded. "Are you nuts? We can't stay here until Sunday! I've already wasted most of my week at that stupid conference, and I've got a board meeting in Chicago tomorrow! The snow is going to stop, and we are leaving first thing in the morning." Amanda took a step backward, and the smile fell from her face. Jim leaned over the desk and said, "Don't bother looking. We only need the room for one night."

Adam looked from Jim to Amanda and smiled. As he checked them in, he said, "Well, if the storm doesn't break or if you decide you'd like to stay, your room is available all weekend."

He handed Jim the keys and gave him directions to the room. He said, "I'll send Sam up in just a few minutes with your bags."

Jim felt flustered, tired, and anxious. His first impression of Adam had been so far off, it was troubling him. He used to be so good at reading people. What had happened? As he began to walk away, he turned back to Adam and said, "Just one more thing, son. How did you know we were out there? It's snowing so hard, you couldn't possibly have seen us until we were right out front. You wouldn't have had time to get your coat on—never mind boots and hat and all."

Adam grinned and said, "Most people wouldn't have noticed that. We have a sensor at the end of the drive that sounds a bell by the desk here when you drive by it. It's just like the bells at the old full-service gas stations."

Jim nodded. "That's pretty clever."

As they made their way to their room, Amanda quietly took in the furnishings and artwork in the hallway. She was angry at Jim, though she doubted he even noticed. She hated it when he talked to her the way he just had in the lobby. And lately, it seemed as if he'd been snapping at her more and more often. Her patience was wearing thin.

Jim was deep in thought. He kept thinking about Adam and his unassuming manner. He was thinking, *If I went to Pritzker, I wouldn't be schlepping luggage in the snow on my vacation.* For some reason, a single word stuck in his mind. He reached into his coat pocket, took out the small leather-bound notebook he carried everywhere, and wrote the word down:

Humility

He didn't write anything else; just the one word. He kept thinking, *Now, why is that stuck in my head?*

"Well, here we are," Amanda said. "Room 329."

Jim inserted the key card in the lock and opened the door.

WARMING UP

The first thing Jim noticed about Room 329 of the Gottschalk Inn was the small gas fireplace on the outside wall. It was lit. The light from the fireplace flickered warmly over a small sitting area near the window.

Amanda stepped into the room from behind him and said, "Wow. That's a nice touch."

Jim said, "Yeah, but I'd hate to see their gas bill."

Looking around the room, Jim had to admit he was somewhat impressed. The room was larger than he expected, and the furnishings were consistent with the rustic lodge feel—but not kitschy. The king-size bed and night tables all appeared to be oak, with simple, clean lines. The bedside lamps as well as a floor lamp in the sitting area had Frank Lloyd Wright–style stained-glass shades over bronzed bases. They were beautiful.

The bed had been turned down, and two chocolates had been left to commemorate the event. The linens were of exceptionally good quality. Jim ran a hand over the sheets and thought they were at least a four-hundred thread count. There was a down duvet and a beautiful coverlet that looked like an old-fashioned quilt. Jim picked up one of the chocolates and noticed a design imprinted on the foil—it looked like a traditional German folk-art design with a heart in the center, surrounded by an intricate geometric pattern. He opened the chocolate and popped it in his mouth; it too was good quality. As he was about to toss the foil into the wastebasket, he noticed printing on the inside. It said: "Trust your heart, as it always speaks the truth." Jim looked at the foil for a moment, folded it in half, and put it in his pocket.

The room had pretty much all the customary trappings of a decent hotel: writing desk, coffee service, ice bucket, and so forth. But just as Amanda was settling into one of the comfortable chairs by the fire, Jim said, "Where's the TV?" Amanda turned to see him looking around the room somewhat frantically, with chocolate still visible on his top lip. "There's no TV!"

Amanda couldn't help herself. Seeing him look so helpless, panicked over a TV, with his hair now a bit disheveled, it struck her as funny. She laughed out loud. "It's okay, dear. I'm sure you'll survive for a night or two without a TV. Adam said the rooms were designed for peace and solitude."

Her laugh hit him like a slap in the face. She really didn't get it. In a manner nearing rage, he turned on her sharply. He glared at her and yelled, "What do you know about what I will or will not survive? You don't even have a job, Amanda! I work my tail off every single day and think about working pretty much every minute when I'm not there. If I want half an hour of television at the end of the day to help numb me into some kind of semblance of sleep, I should be able to have it, goddammit!"

Amanda's face colored as she stood up from her chair by the fire. She felt something boil inside her. Bile rose in her throat, and she narrowed her eyes and practically spat at him when she spoke. "You know what, Jim? I have had just about enough of you talking to me like I'm a piece of dirt. I am not one of your employees! And it's a good thing, because if I was, I'd quit! You may not think I have a *job*, but believe me, if you had to shop and cook and clean and schedule charity engagements and tell your children every day their dad can't get on the phone because he's 'busy'—if you had to do all those things for yourself, you'd appreciate my job." Her voice caught on the last word, and it came out in a sob. Tears rolled over her lashes and onto her cheeks. She was shaking with anger and frustration.

"Oh God, Amanda. I can't take this right now. I'm going to the bar."

He grabbed his key and walked out the door.

Amanda stood there, looking at the empty space in the room where he'd been standing a moment before. It suddenly struck her—there was an empty space in her life that Jim once filled. He assumed it was because she missed the kids. That was partially true. But she now realized what she really missed was him—how he used to be. She knew his work was hard, but something was so different about him since he'd been promoted to COO. He seemed both arrogant and unbelievably insecure at the same time. It was as if he were lost somewhere. Her heart broke for him, for herself, and for the connection that seemed to have been lost between them. She stepped to the window and drew back the curtain. The wind off the frozen lake blew the snow against the windowpane in dancing swirls. The beauty of it touched her. She sat back down and let the tears come.

Jim's frustration made him want to punch the wall. He punched the air in front of him instead and blurted a few choice expletives. He took the stairs down to the first floor and went in search of the lounge. As he neared it, he noticed the business center on his left. He realized he'd forgotten to do the one thing he needed to do in the room—charge his phone. The battery had died just before they found the inn. He thought, *Email first, then a much-needed drink.*

The business center had two fairly new PCs with flat-screen monitors. The desks had an arts-and-crafts design similar to the guest room furniture. He sat down at one of the terminals and clicked the mouse. As the monitor came to life, he noticed the desktop wallpaper was a photo. It was a shot of the sun setting over a lake surrounded by trees in full autumn color. In the foreground of the shot there were beautiful wooden rocking chairs and a round stone fire pit. A glass of wine glimmered in the light from the setting sun. Though he'd never seen the Gottschalk Inn during the day, he knew the photo had been taken there. He secretly admitted it was beautiful.

He clicked on the Internet icon and navigated to the secure portal for his email. He sighed as he logged in. Twenty-seven new emails had arrived since their last stop just a few hours ago. He scrolled through them and answered one from the West Coast office. He looked at his watch. It was 9:26. He figured a few of the die-hard directors in San Francisco would still be in the office. As he was typing out his reply, a new email arrived from the assistant to Milton Wallis.

Milton Wallis was the founder of Wallis International Group and chairman of the board. He'd built the company from just three hotels in Chicago to one of the largest hotel companies in the world. Jim respected him but also thought some of his ideas about hospitality were a bit dated. Jim wanted to focus on capture ratios and the effectiveness of bounce-back offers, and it seemed all Milt wanted to do was talk to Jim about how the product was supposed to make people "feel." Jim usually pawned Milt off on the director of guest services—he just didn't have time to fool with that fluffy stuff.

The email said:

> *To All Board Members and Officers of Wallis International Group:*
>
> *Due to ongoing blizzard conditions in the Chicago area, both O'Hare and Midway Airports have been closed. Furthermore, Interstates 90, 94, and 55 in and around the city are all closed. Lake Shore Drive is currently impassible. City officials are requesting residents stay off the roads and in their homes through tomorrow evening to allow for emergency crews to clear roadways.*
>
> *Because of the severe weather, the meeting of the board of directors has been rescheduled to February 4 and the Chicago offices of Wallis International will be closed tomorrow, Friday, January 16.*
>
> *Zachary Lawson*
Executive Assistant

Jim put his head down next to the keyboard and let out a long, slow breath. Relief! He felt as if it were a stay of execution. This delay bought him two more weeks to come up with a plan for the board. He suddenly loved this storm. He was almost giddy about it. He said aloud to an empty business center, "This calls for a celebratory glass of scotch!"

He logged out of the secure server and strolled down the main corridor to the lounge.

Amanda was unsure how long she'd been sitting when there was a knock at the door. She collected her thoughts and remembered—the bags! Adam was sending Sam up with the bags. She jumped to her feet and yelled, "Just one moment, please!" She ducked into the bathroom and turned on the light. She looked horrible. Her eyes were all red and puffy, her mascara was everywhere, and her nose was runny. She grabbed a tissue and blew her nose. She did her best to wipe off the mess of eye makeup and hoped the porter wouldn't notice how awful she looked as she opened the door.

Standing in the hallway with the bags was a young girl with short, reddish-brown hair who looked about fifteen years old and couldn't have weighed more than a hundred pounds soaking wet. "Hi, Mrs. Watts. I'm Sam! I've brought your bags. May I bring them in for you?"

Amanda was more than a bit surprised Sam the porter was a girl. She said, "Uh . . . um . . . yes, thank you. Of course, please come in." Amanda reached to help the petite young lady with the bags, but Sam said cheerfully, "I've got it, ma'am. I'm stronger than I look!" She proudly lifted both bags with apparent ease and brought them into the room. As she quickly set up two luggage racks and placed the bags on them, she said playfully, in a put-on, movie-announcer voice, "Though she be but little, she is fierce!"

Amanda laughed a little and said, "That's from *A Midsummer Night's Dream*. Do you like Shakespeare?"

As Sam turned to answer her question, she saw Amanda's eyes in the light for the first time. She said somewhat haltingly, "My school did the play . . . just before Christmas. I was Puck." But as she was speaking, a look of concern came over her. She continued by saying, "Are you okay, Mrs. Watts? Is there anything I can do to help you?"

Amanda wiped at her eyes and said, "I'm sure I look horrible. I was hoping you'd be a boy and wouldn't notice my puffy eyes. It's nothing, dear. Mr. Watts and I had a little difference of opinion regarding the lack of a TV in our room, that's all."

"Oh no! Would you like a TV in the room?" Sam practically exclaimed.

"Please don't trouble yourself," Amanda said immediately. But she was astonished at the offer and hesitatingly added, "Would that even be possible?"

Sam, who resembled Shakespeare's impish Puck more and more by the moment, smiled broadly and somewhat mischievously. "Anything is possible at the Gottschalk Inn, Mrs. Watts."

Amanda couldn't help but smile back. "It's Amanda. You can call me Amanda."

"Well, Amanda, you give me ten minutes, and I'll be back with your TV."

Sam returned with a flat-screen TV of modest size but very nice quality. She placed it on a table out of the way but easily visible from both the sitting area and the bed. She chatted merrily as she set up the TV and made certain it worked. It was impossible for Amanda to stay upset with Sam in the room. She was like a little fountain of joy bubbling over. Amanda thought she was, indeed, very much like a little pixie. Before she left the room, Amanda took her hand, tipped her, and said, "Thank you, Sam. I bet you were an excellent Puck."

As Jim walked into the lounge, the first thing he noticed was the bar. It looked about a hundred years old and had beautifully carved mahogany designs and wrought-iron sconces holding lamps that were probably at one time gas but now were electric. His joy from the business center bubbled over, and he said to the man behind the bar, "What a fantastic bar!"

The bartender was a man about Jim's age. He wore jeans and a navy blue flannel shirt. His brown hair was showing signs of gray, and his goatee showed hints as well. He wore reading glasses and was looking at a sheet of paper when Jim walked in, but he took off the glasses to greet him. When he looked up, his eyes were a crystalline blue. They reminded Jim of the photos he'd seen of arctic ice. The bartender smiled and said, "Welcome to the lounge, my friend. I'm Mike."

"Ah, yes—Mike! I understand you're the man I should see about scotch." As he spoke, Jim's eyes widened as he looked more closely at the bottles neatly displayed on either side of the beautiful bar's mirror. What he saw was no amateur selection of scotch. These were the purchases of a connoisseur.

Mike said, "If you're a scotch enthusiast, you've just found your new favorite bar. Have a seat."

"The young man at the desk said you were an expert, but I never thought . . . I mean, I didn't think . . ." Jim stammered a little.

"You didn't think some backwoods lake lover could possibly know what a good glass of scotch was?"

Jim was busted. And he knew it. He turned a little pink and said with a hint of hopelessness in his voice, "I've got a lot to learn, apparently." He thought back to the word he'd written just minutes ago—*Humility*.

Mike laughed out loud, a big booming laugh, and said, "We all do, my friend." He extended his hand and said, "Mike Mueller, nice to meet you."

"Jim Watts." Jim shook hands across the bar and let Mike choose a scotch for him. He delighted in its smooth, smoky finish as they talked.

Jim ran his hands along the well-worn wood of the bar. He said, "I bet this bar could tell a million stories. Like this little indentation here—you think this happened in some long-forgotten bar fight?" He smiled at the thought. "The bar's just beautiful. I'd love to know where the owners found it."

Mike raised one eyebrow, smiled somewhat slyly, and said, "Well, since you're interested, it was my grandfather's. He ran a beer hall and boarding house in Madison back in the early 1900s." He walked from behind the bar and gestured to a black-and-white picture on the wall. In it, there were about a dozen men, almost all with hats and handlebar moustaches. "You see, that's my grandad there, with a bunch of his regular customers, I guess. And as you can see, they're enjoying Wisconsin's finest beer and spirits at this very bar."

Jim stepped over to the wall to look more closely. As he approached Mike and the photo, he noticed a plaque that looked like an old-fashioned tavern sign. It said: "Everyone has a story. Awareness allows us to read it." Jim's gaze shifted from the plaque to the photo. He looked at the picture and then at Mike. He said, "So wait a minute. If that's your grandad, and this was his bar, then . . . you're not just the bartender here."

Mike smiled good-naturedly and said, "See, you're learning already. I am not only the Gottschalk Inn's most skilled bartender and scotch enthusiast—I am also its owner."

Without stopping to think, Jim said, "I would never have guessed you owned or managed a hotel. You seem so happy and content."

"That's spoken like someone who's had some challenges with the hotel business."

Jim shrugged. "I'm not even sure why I said that. I've actually been very successful in this business. I'm COO of Wallis International Group."

Ever so briefly, a look flitted across Mike's face, as if he were going to say something and then changed his mind. He said, "I'm familiar with Wallis. You've got some nice brands of hotels."

"Yes. And if I don't figure out how to get those brands to be more profitable, I'll be applying to work at your front desk with Adam. He's a sharp kid, by the way."

"Adam is sharp. We've got some fantastic people in our little family here. Maybe a few days in the woods will give you some perspective. Perhaps you'll think of something you haven't considered before."

Jim sipped his scotch and said doubtfully, "Perhaps."

Jim had a second drink and visited more with Mike. He was surprised to find they had a lot in common. Mike's business philosophy reminded him a little bit of Milt's, though he decided he was just too tired to debate it tonight.

As Jim finished his drink and settled his tab, Mike said, "I tend to believe there's a purpose to everything in life. Maybe you wound up stuck here for a reason."

"Maybe," Jim said. "Although, if I don't go apologize to my wife, I might not live to find out."

Jim realized the room was mostly dark as he quietly opened the door. There was an odd, bluish light. He thought at first it was the fire, but as he walked into the room, he noticed the fireplace was off. The light was from a TV. A TV! The sound was down, but Jim stood before the TV in amazement. He turned around and looked for Amanda. She was asleep.

As he stood in front of the TV, he noticed a little note on Gottschalk Inn stationery in Amanda's perfect handwriting. It said just one word: "Truce?" It made him laugh a little and smile, and he felt tears well up in his eyes. To stem the tide of tears he felt coming, he sighed a bit and stuck his hands in his pockets—as he used to do as a kid anytime he felt uncomfortable. Amid the coins and his receipt from the bar, his hand brushed the foil from the chocolate. He didn't even have to take it out to recall its message. He whispered, "Trust your heart, as it always speaks the truth."

He walked over and sat on the bed next to Amanda. *She looks the same*, he thought. That is, she looked the same as the day he'd summoned every ounce of his courage and asked her out. He reached out and stroked her hair.

"Mandy. Mandy, honey, wake up a minute."

Amanda stretched a little and opened her eyes. She couldn't remember the last time he'd called her Mandy. She said through a yawn, "Do you like your present?"

"It's amazing! How did you do that? It doesn't even seem possible!"

"Well, as I learned from Sam, the porter, tonight, apparently anything is possible at the Gottschalk Inn."

"You mean a porter brought us a TV? That's incredible. The quality of the execution here is really something."

"Not just any porter. Sam—as in Samantha—the seventeen-year-old girl, magic fairy porter. I agree the execution is amazing, honey, but there's something else going on here. It's like electricity or a magic spell all around the place."

"You're right. This place and everyone in it seems to just have this unbelievable energy. That sounds so unlike me to say, but I can't for the life of me figure out how else to explain it."

As Jim described what he was thinking, Amanda saw a change come across his face. The lines and edges smoothed, and his eyes softened. He lay down next to her, clothes and all. He buried his face in her hair, which smelled of sandalwood and citrus, and said, "Mandy, I'm so sorry. Please forgive me. I feel like I'm failing. I feel like a hamster on one of those wheels—I'm working so hard all the time, but I'm not getting anywhere. I've been so scared and angry all the time, and I've been taking it all out on you."

She turned to him and touched his face as she said, "You're not going to fail, Jim. You're the most brilliant hotelier and businessperson I know. And you've got me on your side. But we can save the world tomorrow. For now, let's get some sleep."

Jim got up to change. As he took his notebook out of his pocket, he opened it and wrote the following two words:

$$\text{Energy + Execution}$$

He looked out the window and couldn't see much except the storm still raging away. He placed his notebook on the table by the bed, assuming he'd wake up two or three times in the night with thoughts racing, as he normally did. He climbed into the warm and comfortable bed beside Amanda, who'd forgiven him, and fell into a deep sleep.

Waking Up

Jim rolled over, stretched, and yawned broadly. He rubbed his eyes and looked at the clock by the bed. It said 8:14. He sat up abruptly and looked around for Amanda. She was sitting by the fireplace with a book.

"Holy cow—did I just sleep through the whole night? I can't even remember the last time that happened!"

Amanda chuckled at him. "Apparently you did. How does it feel?"

Jim relaxed a bit and grinned back. "It feels wonderful, actually. Maybe this place does have a little magic."

He took a moment to collect his thoughts and then said, "Did I tell you last night that the board meeting today is cancelled? Apparently the weather in the city was even worse than it was here. They've closed the offices until Monday, and Milt rescheduled the meeting to next month."

She looked at him and sighed relief. "Well, that's good. You're way overdue for a day off."

"You're right. This job has been making me nuts. Maybe a day off will do me some good. I'm sorry again I've been so miserable to you, Mandy. I don't know why you put up with me, but I'm so glad you do."

She raised her hand to silence him. "You said everything that needed to be said last night—and you put up with me, too, by the way." She got up and kissed him on the forehead and smoothed out the fading sleep lines from his cheek. "How about a little coffee, Mr. Watts?"

"That sounds fantastic."

While Amanda brewed them both coffee, Jim pulled on his sweats and made a half-hearted effort to smooth his hair. He walked to the window and marveled at the spectacle outside. The bright daylight and clear sky revealed the intensity of the storm. Where the tall pines fringed the lake, Jim could see several had fallen from either the wind or the sheer weight of the snow. It looked as if two or three feet of snow had fallen. Against every structure facing the lake, there were massive drifts where the wind had piled the snow. And in the morning sunlight, everything sparkled.

"Wow. That was some storm. I can't believe I slept through so much of it."

Amanda stepped up beside him and handed him a cup of coffee. She sipped her own and said, "It's just gorgeous. It makes me want to go outside and play!"

Jim laughed and said, "We're going to go out and play, all right. We're going to play a fun game called 'help Jim dig the car out.' But first, let's go find something to eat. I'm ravenous."

Thirty minutes later, Jim and Amanda entered the small restaurant adjacent the lounge. "Honey, come look at this awesome old bar over here," Jim said as he walked Amanda through the small dining area to the semi-dark lounge. There were a few guests in the restaurant, and as they walked through, a tall, cheerful-looking woman said, "Good morning! You must be Mr. and Mrs. Watts. I'm Wendy; please make yourselves at home."

Jim and Amanda looked at each other with eyebrows raised and then turned back to Wendy. "How did you know who we are?" Amanda asked. She was sure she'd never seen this woman before. But looking more closely, Amanda thought there was something familiar about Wendy—something about her eyes in particular, which were what made her seem so cheery.

"Not too much that happens at the Gottschalk Inn gets by me. I've got connections." And she winked.

Jim laughed and said almost apologetically, "I was just going to show my wife the antique bar before we sit."

Wendy smiled and said, "Of course! Take your time. That bar is Mike's pride and joy. You won't find a speck of dust on it, that's for sure."

Amanda decided she liked this woman. There was something about her—confident, a bit sassy, and completely charming.

Jim walked Amanda over to the bar and began pointing out the distinctive features, like a tour guide. "I met Mike last night. He's not only the bartender and a scotch lover, like me—he's also the owner of this inn. This came from a beer hall his grandad owned up in Madison in the early 1900s. Isn't it great?" Jim took her hand as he spoke and guided it along the smooth, well-worn wood of the bar top.

Amanda looked at Jim and saw genuine enthusiasm in his face. *What a difference twenty-four hours and a good night's sleep can make*, she thought. His energy was infectious, and she soon saw the mastery and beauty of the old bar.

She said, "It's amazing the craftsmanship that goes into something like this. I can't imagine how long it took to create all those pieces."

As she gestured toward the intricately carved shelves and posts, the lights came on in the lounge. A voice from behind them said, "I know you enjoy a good scotch, my friend, but it's a tad early, isn't it?"

Jim made no effort to conceal his pleasure at hearing Mike's voice. He turned and said, "Mike! Good morning! So good to see you! Honey, this is Mike, who I was just talking about! Mike, meet Amanda, my wife."

Mike took Amanda's hand and shook it warmly. He met her eyes and said, "So nice to meet you. I hope you're finding our little inn comfortable."

"Oh, it's just fabulous! Everything is so lovely, and your staff is just fantastic! Adam at the front desk was so helpful, and I want to take Sam, the magic porter, home with me! She's just phenomenal. You must be very proud."

"I am proud. I'm proud of all of them. Every person here has unique gifts that add value to the team. More than anything, we just encourage them to be themselves and stay aware and focused on what's happening in the moment. And I agree; it is hard to resist Miss Sam's charm." He gestured toward the dining room, where Wendy was bustling about between tables. "I think Wendy might put up a fight if you try to take her home, though. She's Sam's mom."

Amanda exclaimed, "I thought she looked familiar! Now I see the resemblance completely. I don't know how I missed it!"

Jim said, "I'm looking forward to meeting this Sam. My wife swears she's a magic fairy. Apparently, she conjured us a TV out of thin air last night." As Jim said that, he realized he had completely forgot to turn on the TV while he was getting dressed. Normally, he didn't like to miss the news, but this morning, he hadn't even thought of it.

Mike smiled and said, "That's our Sam. She knows anything is possible at the Gottschalk Inn."

"We keep hearing that," Jim said. "Right now, I'm ready for someone to make breakfast possible. I'm hungry!"

"We can certainly make that happen. Let me show you to a nice table by the windows, and Wendy will fix you right up. Maybe after breakfast, you'd like to spend a little time outside? It's a beautiful day." As he spoke, Mike walked them to a sunny table by the big windows overlooking the lake.

"I don't know about getting outside," Jim said. "We've got boots in the car, but I think I'm going to have to borrow a shovel to dig it out."

"Well, how about you borrow some snowshoes or cross-country skis instead? Your car is already dug out. Billy took care of that for you first thing this morning."

"You're kidding! Really? That's incredible! You've really got something special going on here, Mike." Jim was impressed.

Amanda chimed in and said, "Snowshoes! You have snowshoes we can borrow? Oh, Jim, we haven't been snowshoeing in ages. Let's do it!" Her excitement at the idea was palpable.

Mike nodded to Jim in reply and then turned to Amanda. "There's a nice little trail that goes up along the lakeshore. About a mile out, there's a rocky overlook that's got a million-dollar view. It'll be nice and quiet on the trail today, and the weather is supposed to stay clear now. Anyway, it sounds like the roads in Chicago are still a big mess from the storm."

Amanda looked at Jim expectantly. He looked out the window at the lake and could faintly see the trail cutting into the dense trees. He suddenly relished the idea of getting outside and hiking among those trees. He imagined himself standing

in the woods in the dappled sunlight and breathing deeply
the pine-scented air. He looked at Amanda, whose eyes were
shining with anticipation. He then looked at Mike and said
with a smile, "Your little Sam isn't the only source of magic
around here. Who can resist my wife's enthusiasm?"

Amanda bounced up and down on her seat and clapped
her hands. "Yay! We're going outside!" she said girlishly.

Her joy made Mike smile. He said, "Whenever you're
ready, just call down or stop by the front desk and let them
know. Billy will get you outfitted and show where to pick up
the trail. And for now, I'll leave you in Wendy's very capable
hands to enjoy your breakfast." He patted Jim on the shoulder,
leaned in, and smiled mischievously. "I'm glad you lived." He
then reached over to take Amanda's hand. "It's a pleasure to
meet you, Amanda."

"Mike, the pleasure is all mine," she replied with sincerity.

Mike wasn't gone thirty seconds when Wendy appeared
with a pot of coffee in hand. "Who's ready for a little caffeine
therapy?"

Both Jim and Amanda laughed and raised their hands as if
answering a teacher's question in grade school. There was something about Wendy that commanded that kind of response.

As Wendy poured the coffee and handed them menus,
Amanda said, "Mike told us you're Sam's mom. I just adore
her. She's bright and funny and charming. You must be a
great mom."

Wendy smiled proudly and said without a hint of irony,
"You know what, I *am* a great mom. It helps to have good kids,
though." She pulled a photo from her apron pocket and set it
on the table. "Sammie's the oldest of my four. This is Megan;
she's fourteen. Sarah is ten, and my little man there, Ian, is
eight. They drive me a little crazy sometimes, but they're mine,
and I love 'em all to pieces."

Jim noticed that when Wendy spoke, it was impossible not to give her your full attention. She stood up straight and spoke with conviction. There was absolutely no nonsense or pretense to Wendy. He liked that.

"Wendy, I am as hungry as a goat. What do you recommend?"

"Well, Eva's in the kitchen today, and she's pretty much the best cook I've ever met in my life. In fact, my kids all want her to come live with us. The Midwest omelet is incredible. It's got onions and peppers with apple-smoked bacon and Wisconsin cheddar cheese. And the homemade banana-bread French toast is like falling in love with every bite." Wendy waited a moment and saw Jim and Amanda turn their eyes to the menus to deliberate. She said, "I'll give you a few minutes to decide. If you have any questions, just let me know."

She stepped away from the table, and Jim and Amanda took a moment to peruse the menus and sip their coffees. As she moved through the dining room, a gentleman sitting alone flagged her down. He appeared to be in his mid-seventies, and Jim couldn't help notice the frustration in his voice. "Wendy! Look at this bacon!" he said huffily. He picked up a piece of bacon and waved it at her. "I like my bacon extra crispy, and this is *not* extra crispy!"

"Okay, Frank, you got it. Let me take care of that for you." She reached out to take the offending side of bacon away, and he practically slapped her hand.

"I don't want you to take it! I'm hungry, and I'll eat it the way it is. It's just damned frustrating, that's what it is! Damned frustrating! I've been here a half a dozen times now, and you'd think someone would remember how I like my bacon!" He was practically growling. "And I want more coffee!"

Jim thought, *Oh, here we go . . . I've seen this a thousand times.* He thought of Wendy's almost brusque, no-nonsense approach and figured she'd be handing this guy a piece of her mind any minute. *Well, even the Gottschalk Inn isn't perfect*, he said to himself. But then he felt a bit guilty because he was almost relieved at the thought.

Wendy said nothing else at the moment but brought Frank more coffee and put her hand on his shoulder as she poured it. Jim expected to see him jump and recoil at her touch, but the old man's shoulders actually sagged a little. She rubbed his shoulder a bit and leaned over and said something too softly for anyone but him to hear. Jim was surprised to see the old man nod and take a deep breath, which he let out with a sigh.

Wendy came back to the table and took their order. After looking over the menu, which offered a nice variety of breakfast basics as well as a few more sophisticated choices, Jim and Amanda decided to follow Wendy's recommendations.

The food arrived quickly and was hot and absolutely delicious. Amanda agreed every bite of her French toast was a little bit like falling in love. Jim ate his omelet with gusto, and in the pleasure of his meal, he forgot about the curious old gentleman. When he finally looked up from his plate, the man was gone.

Jim and Amanda left their sunny table by the window with full stomachs and content minds. They meandered to the lobby and looked out front to the parking area. Mike was right. Their car and every other car in the lot had been shoveled out and cleared off. The lot was plowed, and the main walkways cleared. Though he was wearing only a sweater, Jim decided to dash out to the car and get their snow boots.

Amanda made herself comfortable in one of the chairs by the big fireplace. The lobby looked so different in the daytime. It was flooded with sunlight, and the wooden beams seemed to absorb the light and glow from within.

While she was sitting in the high-backed chair, Amanda heard Wendy's voice behind her. She turned sideways to thank Wendy again for the phenomenal breakfast but stopped herself short before she spoke. Wendy was standing face to face with the grumpy older man from the dining room. Amanda couldn't see his face, but she could see Wendy's, and it was filled with both compassion and concern. Amanda turned back around, not wanting to disturb them. But she could plainly hear their conversation.

"I'm sorry, Wendy, dear. I had no business snapping at you like that. No business at all."

"Aw, Frank, you know I love ya, no matter what. Don't you give it another thought."

"Well, you're an awfully sweet girl. I'm a little upset today, you know. I was hoping I could get to Minnesota by the weekend, and they're having another big storm push through as we speak."

"And how is he this week, Frank? Any improvement?" Wendy's voice was filled with tenderness.

"No, my dear. We don't expect any improvement now. I think it's probably down to days or weeks now—not months any longer."

"Oh, hon, I hate to hear that. I buried my brother a few years back, and I don't care how old you are—it's just a very hard thing. You're a good man, Frank, to drive all that way so often to be with him."

"Well, even if it's the best cancer center in the world, it's still a hospital. And even though he's seventy, he's still my kid brother. I just can't leave him alone over there."

"You're a good brother. When you get there, you give him some love from us, okay? That new storm is supposed to stay south of us here. I bet it will be over and done with in Minnesota by morning, and you can get back on the road. And in the meantime, Frank, you let me know if there's anything I can do for you. I'm off at three today, and if you'd like, we can sit out here by the fire and play a game or two of chess before I head on home."

"Oh, thank you, you sweet girl. But you get home to those children when you're done. I'll be just fine here."

"You hang in there, Frank. I'm going to send you off with a big hug to tide you over."

Amanda heard them embrace and part ways. As she heard their footsteps retreating, she stood, amazed at the exchange. As she turned away from the fireplace to face the lobby, she saw Jim, who'd been standing near the coffee service, apparently pretending to look at an old framed map of the lake on the wall. When he turned toward her, his face told her he'd heard Wendy and Frank's conversation, too. His expression was full of wonder, and there were tears in his eyes.

As they walked backed to their room, Jim heard Mike's voice echo in his head: "Every person here has unique gifts that add value to the team. More than anything, we just encourage them to be themselves and stay aware and focused on what's happening in the moment."

As they entered the room, Jim picked up his notepad and wrote another word:

Awareness

He finally remembered to plug his phone into the charger, and they began to change into their warm outdoor clothes.

CONNECTING

Ready to hit the trail, Jim and Amanda went to the lobby to meet Billy. They'd called down, and he was waiting for them when they arrived. He looked hearty—dressed in insulated coveralls and a bright orange ski cap. His cheeks were red from the cold. When he greeted them, he smiled with his whole person. With an accent Jim couldn't quite place, he said, "Jim and Amanda—hi there! I'm Billy. You guys ready for a little outdoor adventure? It's a perfect day for it!"

"We are so ready!" Amanda replied.

"I'm as ready as I'm going to be," Jim said. "When I get too tired, Amanda can carry me."

She shoved his shoulder like a teenager. "Come on, tough guy. You can do it!"

Billy laughed and said, "Now kids, no fighting. Let's head out to the warming house and get you set up."

They walked just around the side of the lodge to a quaint little building with a heater and benches. Billy opened a large storage area that had a variety of skiing, snowshoeing, and ice fishing equipment. He looked over both Jim and Amanda and chose snowshoes and poles appropriate for their sizes and weights. He showed them how to adjust the straps on the snowshoes and handed Jim a small map of the trail. The same map was displayed on the wall. He walked them both over and said, "I'll take you to the trailhead, and if I was you, I'd follow this trail right here, keeping the lake to your right as you go out. It's kind of a climb, but if you guys come back along the same route, it will be a wicked nice downhill hike on the way back."

Jim looked at him and said, "'Wicked nice'? You're not from Wisconsin."

"Nah. I grew up in Boston. My grandfather was army buddies with Mike's dad in World War II. As a kid, we used to come out here every summer, and I just fell in love with the whole place. Mike's dad built it after the war, and my grandpa helped—he built the big stone fireplace in the lobby. Mike's like an uncle to me, and when I got laid off a couple a years ago, he offered me a job here at the inn. He's good people—he's a *wicked* good guy," Billy said with a chuckle, emphasizing his Boston accent. "I owe him a lot."

"So, is that why you guys have such a nice thing going here—because you're actually all related?" Jim said, then thinking to himself, *It may work here, but it would never work at Wallis.*

Billy looked thoughtful for a moment. "You know," he said, "actually only Wendy and Sam are related. There's a funny thing that happens at the Gottschalk Inn, though, and I think it's always been that way: You don't work here because you're family. You become family because you work here. It's the place that makes us a family, not the genes."

Billy brought Jim and Amanda outside to a bench. He helped them get into their snowshoes and stepped into a pair of his own. He hiked them around to the back side of the inn and down by the lake. He brought them to the opening in the trees Jim had seen from the room. The snow was deep, but the snowshoes made moving much easier.

"Should be a nice hike out. If you're up for it, about a mile or so out is a super-nice overlook. You'll know when you get there. I'll be here all day, so I'll see you when you get back. Have fun!" With that, Billy turned back toward the inn and left them on their own.

Jim and Amanda plodded along the trail in silence. The sound of their snowshoes crunching through the pristine snow on the trail and the sound of their breathing was all they could hear. Occasionally, the breeze would blow a shower of dusty snow through the trees, creating a swirl of glitter around them and above their heads. It was breathtakingly beautiful. It filled them both with a sense of reverence.

Amanda was physically fit. She and Jim used to hike together all the time when they and the kids were younger. She still walked along Lake Michigan when the weather cooperated and took yoga classes two or three times a week. Jim, though still trim, was noticing his breathing was a bit heavier than he expected, and he had to push himself when the trail sloped upward. He'd stopped working out regularly when he'd been promoted to COO. Most days, it seemed he didn't have time—and on the days he did have time, he just didn't have the energy. A bit ahead of him, Amanda stopped and waited for him to catch up. She reached into the pocket of her jacket and pulled out a bottle of water. She took a few swigs and passed the bottle to Jim, who took it gratefully.

"I'm out of shape. My body is yelling at me for not working out," Jim said.

"Well, the snow is deep, so even with good snowshoes, even a short trek is a workout. I'm feeling it in my legs, for sure. Let's rest a while when we get to the overlook."

"I hope we're close. The trail is steadily climbing now, so I bet we are. Let's do this!" And with renewed energy and determination, Jim forged ahead of Amanda.

A short while later, they crested a fairly steep hill, and the trees gave way to a clearing. They knew instantly they'd reached the overlook. Mike was right: it was a million-dollar view. They were easily sixty feet above the shore and could see almost the entire lake, skirted by pine woods and dotted here and there with homes, several of which sent up thin, wispy trails of wood smoke from chimneys. The lake was completely frozen and now covered with snow. On the far side of the lake, they could just barely make out a few clusters of ice fishing houses. The breeze in the clearing brought them the scent of pine and someone's nearby wood fire. Jim closed his eyes and inhaled deeply. The air that filled his lungs was cool and clean. It felt like a long drink of water on a hot day.

It had taken them longer than they thought to reach the overlook. The sun was high, but it was clearly past noon. Jim used his arms to clear the snow from a big flat-topped rock so they could sit and rest awhile. They unfastened their snowshoes and sat for a few minutes, catching their breath and finishing the water. As Jim polished off the last of it, Amanda said, "We probably should have brought more water—we won't have any for the hike back."

She was right. Jim couldn't believe he hadn't thought to bring any. A mile had sounded like such a short hike, but in January, in deep snow, a mile was a challenge. "Well, at least going back, the trail slopes downward—that should help."

Amanda pulled her hood up and lay back on the rock. Looking upward, she could see the tops of the trees around the clearing, swaying, almost dancing, as the breeze passed through. The sky was crystal clear, and the sun warmed her face. "Oh, honey, this is awesome. You've got to do this."

Jim shifted and lay back alongside her. The big rock was more comfortable than he expected. It felt good to stretch his abdominal muscles, and the sun quickly began to dry the sweat from his forehead and neck. He closed his eyes and almost felt as though he could nap right there. The deep snow muffled all the sounds of the woods, with the exception of the wind coming off the lake. The breeze wasn't strong or too cold. It just blew through the trees, making a sound a little like the waves of the ocean rolling onto the beach.

Jim felt his mind quiet down and clear. He suddenly felt overwhelmed with gratitude. He thought about his life, about Amanda and the kids, about his work and Milt—and he felt so fortunate for all of it. He reached over and took Amanda's mitten-covered hand and gave it a gentle squeeze, which she returned.

He said, "I feel like I'm here on purpose, as if the storm and everything that got us here is all because I'm supposed to learn something at this place. Does that sound crazy?"

"I don't think that sounds crazy at all. You know I've always believed things happen for a reason, even if we don't understand what the reason is right away."

"Now you sound like Mike. He said almost the same thing last night. Everything about this place is extraordinary. It seems like everyone here is connected—they're like a family. And they all seem to adore Mike. I just keep thinking, if I could find a way to get even half of the employees at Wallis to create what this little quirky team is creating at the Gottschalk Inn, no one would be able to touch us. We'd book out every property, every night."

"Well, why can't you?"

"I've got ten thousand employees all over the world. Mike has—what? Two dozen or so? And they all seem to be connected to each other."

"Well, maybe that's the secret."

"What's the secret?"

"Being connected to one another. Maybe that's what makes this team so special—the relationships they have with one another. Maybe if you create an environment where the employees love and trust one another, then they can really connect with your guests on a new level. Maybe that's what you should focus on at Wallis."

Jim rolled onto his side and propped himself up on his elbow. He looked at her thoughtfully and said, "Maybe you're right. But how?"

She smiled and said, "You've been married to me for twenty-eight years, James Watts. You should know by now that I'm always right." She grinned from ear to ear and gave him her sassiest look.

"Is that so? Well, you may be right. But I've got stealth— like a ninja. . . ." And with no warning at all, he rolled her off the rock into the fluffy deep snow as she laughed and shrieked. He roared with laughter as she got up. She was completely covered with snow.

She wiped the snow from her face and said, "Oh, you've done it now, Mr. Ninja. You're going down!" She lunged at him and shoved him off the rock. Within seconds, snow was flying, and they were both darting about the clearing, throwing snow at one another and laughing like children.

An unusual noise broke the spell. They both stopped and looked at one another with puzzlement. Neither one could place the sound, but it was a manmade one—not a natural one.

Amanda said, "A chainsaw? Could someone be cutting a fallen tree?"

Jim replied, "Doubtful in all this snow. It's an engine, though, for sure." Then it dawned on him. "Of course! It's a snowmobile!" The words were barely out of his mouth when they saw a black and silver snowmobile coming up the trail from the direction of the inn. The driver stopped in the clearing. With the helmet and thick snow clothes, it was impossible to tell who it was until the driver stood up and stepped away from the sled. The tiny build gave it away.

"Sam!" Amanda hollered.

Sam removed her helmet and bowed, as if on stage. "Miss Samantha Parker, at your service. I bring you tidings from the Gottschalk Inn." When she stood up, she cocked her head to one side like a bird, raised her eyebrows, and said, "Uh, am I interrupting something? You two look like a polar expedition gone very, very wrong." Sam looked quizzically at the pair standing knee-deep in snow—they were half-soaked, with hair and hats askew, snow packed into the zippers of their coats and their cuffs.

Jim and Amanda looked at each other and just started laughing again. They looked ridiculous, and they both had tears running down their cheeks from laughter. It felt great. Amanda pointed teasingly at Jim and said, "He started it! He shoved me off the rock into the snow!"

Jim laughed and said, "I was provoked! It was irresistible, really—she set me up perfectly." He stepped toward Sam and said, "I'm just delighted I finally get to meet Sam, the magic porter, who can conjure TVs from thin air." Jim shook most of the snow from his gloves before shaking Sam's hand.

"Well, if you liked that trick, I think you'll really applaud for this one." She opened the compartment under the seat of the snowmobile and removed a backpack. While presenting the pack to Jim with a deep bow and a grand flourish, she said,

"Do you think because you are virtuous, that there will be no more cakes and ale?"

Amanda shook her head and said, "Last night it was *A Midsummer Night's Dream*, now the pixie quotes *Twelfth Night*."

Sam smiled at her and said, "Wow. You really know your Shakespeare."

Amanda said, "Well, I used to teach. And speaking of which, today's Friday. Shouldn't you be in school?"

Sam raised her arms and opened them high above her and did a little dance. "It's a snow day! I love snow days! So, since I was just sitting at home, Mike, in all his awesomeness, let me come in for a few hours this afternoon."

While Sam and Amanda talked, Jim opened up the backpack. "Honey, they sent us lunch!" The pack had bottled water, a thermos of coffee, sandwiches, fruit, and brownies for dessert.

"A little something for the polar explorers from Eva and my mom. My mom fixed the coffee the way she saw you fix it this morning—cream and a little sweetener, right?"

Jim looked astonished. "That's right! You really *are* magic! Thank you, Sam."

"You are very welcome. And truth be told, I'm always psyched to volunteer for errands that involve Mike's new sled. This thing is awesome!"

Jim asked, "Mike lets you take his personal snowmobile out on the trail? That's pretty nice."

"Yes, it is. But he trusts me, so I take good care of it. If you want to be trusted, you've got to be trustworthy. That's what my mom always says." She stepped onto the board of the snowmobile and started it up. "I'll leave you two to enjoy your lunch!"

With that, she zipped off down the trail, and the peace and silence of the woods enveloped them once more.

In the pack was also a plastic-backed blanket they laid over the rock. They sat cross-legged and ate their sandwiches, which were delicious, and drank their coffee while their hats and gloves dried off in the sun. The food was delicious. Jim thought about their earlier conversation and said, "You know what, Mandy? You really are right about Wallis. I've been focusing on the wrong things. I've spent so much time looking at the numbers, I've forgotten to look at the people." He held his sandwich up to her and said, "Think about this sandwich. . . ."

Amanda looked at him and thought for a moment she'd hit him a little too hard with one of those snowballs. She said with her mouth still partly full, "What about it—other than the fact that it's totally amazing? Is that chipotle mayo, you think?"

Jim said, "No, Amanda, seriously. Think of what it took to get this sandwich to us out here on the trail. Someone we've never met ordered the food and paid for it. Eva, who we only know by name, made it. Wendy packed it and remembered how we take our coffee. And Sam delivered it. Billy had to tell her where we were. And Mike made it all possible by creating a climate where all of those people work together seamlessly. Because they have such extraordinary relationships with one another, we now have a relationship with every single person involved in that transaction—even the ones behind the scenes. This sandwich tells a story."

Amanda had stopped eating and stared at him. "You're right. We are connected by an invisible thread to all those people. And it's part of why we're falling in love with this place."

Jim lowered his voice and said earnestly, "I *can* make Wallis a place where people feel connected. I know I can. And when they're connected to one another and to the organization, they will be able to connect to our guests. And the numbers will improve. I just know it."

Amanda loved the way his face beamed as he spoke. She could see the intensity she'd always loved about him, but now there was also optimism behind it. She leaned over and kissed him full on the lips.

The kiss brought him back to the moment. He met her eyes, smiled, and said, "We have to hike more often."

They took their time on the trail heading back to the inn, and the afternoon sun was getting low when they stepped into the warming house. Billy was there, as promised, and took their gear. He said, "You guys look awesome. You're both all rosy! Did you have a good time?"

They both nodded, but Jim spoke first. "What a beautiful trail! We had a great day. And the lunch was such a nice surprise. It showed up like magic!"

"Well, you know anything is possible . . ." Billy began to say, then both Jim and Amanda chimed in with him ". . . at the Gottschalk Inn." Billy laughed and said, "So you're gettin' the picture! Anyway, Sammie loves to drive Mike's sled. She was happy to help out on that one."

Jim patted Billy on the back and said playfully, "Well, Billy, we had a *wicked* good time!"

Billy laughed and said, "Now you sound like you're from my old neighborhood. You sure we're not cousins?"

Jim laughed in reply and said, "Maybe? Who knows!"

As Jim and Amanda made their way back to the room, they passed by the restaurant, which was now very quiet. Jim touched Amanda on the arm and said, "Come with me for a minute."

As they passed through the nearly empty restaurant, Jim noticed Wendy off to the side of the dining room. She was cleaning the area where the service ware and beverages were kept. As he stepped up to her, she turned as if she sensed them there and said, "Hey guys, how was the hike?"

"Oh, it was fantastic," Jim said. "Thank you, Wendy. Say, I wanted to ask you a favor."

"Sure! What can I do for you?"

"Since the restaurant is slow right now, do you think Amanda and I could see the kitchen and meet Eva?"

"Of course you can! Come on, I'll introduce you."

Wendy walked them both into the kitchen, which was brightly lit and immaculately clean and well organized. An older woman in a chef's white coat was leaning over a large stainless-steel work table and looking over what appeared to be some kind of invoice or report with a young man. She had short, cropped silver hair and olive skin. She looked up, and Jim noticed she had deep-set dark brown eyes. She touched the young man on the shoulder and said quietly, "Good job, Kurt—you can finish the rest on your own. You've got this." He nodded and walked away.

Wendy said, "Hey, Eva, this is Jim and Amanda from Chicago. They wanted to see the kitchen and meet you."

Eva gestured around her and said, "Well, this is it! It's not fancy, but it works for us."

Amanda said, "It's so clean! And your food is just amazing."

They chatted for a few minutes about the menu and the kitchen staff. Eva showed them around proudly. As the brief tour wound down, Jim said, "Eva, I want to talk to you about the sandwiches you sent us today."

Eva's face darkened a bit. She said, "Oh no, was there something wrong?"

"Oh, goodness, no!" Jim said. "They were wonderful. What I want to say is thank you—it may sound foolish, but I learned something about my own business today because of the sandwich you made. And that wouldn't have happened if you hadn't put love and care and pride into making it."

"Well, you're welcome. I can't take the credit. I have an amazing crew of young people in here."

"Well, even the most extraordinary crew only thrives with great leadership."

Eva looked thoughtful and said, "Would you mind if I asked what it was you learned? From the sandwich, I mean?"

Jim laughed a little and said, "That must sound a little nuts, huh? You taught me today that every one of my employees has a relationship with my guests. Whether they are paying the bills, doing the laundry, or making sandwiches, the people behind the scenes are just as much a part of guest service as the ones at the front desk. I learned that in this business, a sandwich isn't just a sandwich."

Eva looked at him for what felt like a long time. Then she said quietly, "Thank you. I can't tell you what that means to me."

Jim took her hand and said, "No, thank you."

They parted ways, and Jim and Amanda returned to their room to rest and change before dinner. As Jim peeled off his warm layers, he noticed his notebook on the table by the bed. He sat down and looked at what he'd written so far:

Humility

Energy + Execution

Awareness

He'd known since talking with Amanda over lunch out on the trail what he'd be adding next to his notebook. He wrote the following word, in all capital letters:

RELATIONSHIPS

He set the notebook back down and joined Amanda, who was warming herself by the fire. They decided to enjoy a quiet Friday night together and ordered a simple dinner in the room.

THE LESSON

Saturday morning dawned bright. Jim woke to the faint sound of whirring off in the distance, but he couldn't quite place it. He and Amanda enjoyed their coffee in the comfort of the room. Amanda opened the inner curtains and said, "Another gorgeous day. I'm so happy we stayed. Thank you."

"Thank you for suggesting it," Jim replied. "I haven't slept this well in ages."

She turned from the window. "You know what I'm thinking about right now?"

Jim looked at her and said, "Midwest omelet?"

"Close. I'm more of a French toast girl. Let's go eat."

As they turned the corner from the hallway to the restaurant, they both opened their eyes wide. The quiet little restaurant from yesterday morning was absolutely hopping. Every table in both the restaurant and lounge was filled, and the level of activity and chatter made it seem like a beehive.

Wendy bustled by with a big tray of food and said, "Good morning, Jim and Amanda. I'll be right with you."

Mike was also busy at the bar, sending out Bloody Marys and mimosas. He looked up as they came in, and he smiled at the astonished looks on their faces. Jim scanned the room and looked carefully at the faces of the customers. Everyone seemed happy. A young man bussed tables quickly and efficiently. Wendy and two other servers practically danced from table to table, filling coffee and waters and chatting happily as they took orders, delivered steaming plates of food, and checked in with their guests.

Jim also noticed something unusual about the restaurant guests—many of them had what looked like motorcycle jackets on the backs of their chairs and helmets by their feet. Some of them wore snow pants unzipped to the hip. Jim's eyes looked beyond the guests to the windows and realized for the first time what that whirring sound had been—snowmobiles. Dozens of them—all parked down by the lake in tidy rows.

Wendy stepped up to greet them and said, "Well, good morning! What do you think of our Sled Dogs?"

"Excuse me?" Jim said.

"Our snowmobile crowd—this group comes in every Saturday as long as there's snow. They call themselves the Sled Dogs. Quite a sight, isn't it?"

"It certainly is. How long have they been doing this?"

"Well, let's see . . . see that older gentleman over there? That's Walt. He's one of the originals. He's been riding out here since the very beginning—sometime in the mid-'60s."

"Wow. So he's been coming to the Gottschalk Inn all that time?"

"Sure has. In fact, Walt used to work here as a kid. He worked for Mike's dad in the early days."

"Oh man. I'd love to talk with him, but I'd hate to disturb his breakfast."

"Are you kidding me? You give Walt a chance to reminisce about the old days, and he'll be your pal for life. Let me introduce you."

"Seriously? That would be amazing!"

"Follow me." Wendy walked Jim and Amanda over to Walt's table, where he was sitting with a woman. They both appeared to be in their late sixties or early seventies. "Hi there, Walt! There's someone who would like to meet you. This is Jim Watts from Chicago and his wife, Amanda. Jim's a big shot in the hotel business with Wallis International, and he'd like to ask you some questions about the old days. Jim, this is Walter Birger, and this is his girlfriend, Mary."

Walt and Mary both looked up from their conversation. There was something youthful about them both, despite their age. Walt's hair was pure white, and he had a perfectly groomed white mustache to match. His eyes were pale blue and seemed to smile. Walt said, "Well, hello there! It's a pleasure to meet you both. Why don't you join us? We've got the best server in the house!" Walt gestured to the two empty seats at their table and then winked at Wendy as she went back to the bustle of the dining room.

"Are you sure you don't mind?" Amanda said. "We'd hate to interrupt your breakfast."

Mary spoke up and said, "Of course we don't mind. We love to meet new people, and Walt's always happy to tell a few stories about the old days."

"In that case, we would love to! Thank you so much," Jim said. He pulled out a chair for Amanda and then sat down himself. "I'm ready for some of Wendy's caffeine therapy!"

As if on cue, Wendy reappeared with a steaming pot of coffee and filled their cups. She said, "I'll give you some time to visit and then come back and take your order."

Amanda said, "Actually, we're going to make it really easy—we're going to have the same things we ate yesterday. Is that boring?"

"It's not boring if it makes you happy. Order what you like. So, Midwestern omelet for Jim and banana-bread French toast for you?"

"Very good! I'm amazed you can remember with so much going on!"

"I'm a trained professional—do not try this at home!" she said with a flourish that made Amanda see where Sam's flair originated.

As Wendy walked away, Jim and Amanda's attention shifted back to Walt and Mary. Jim said, "Walt, Wendy tells me you used to work here back in the early days of the inn. Is that true?"

"Oh, yes. I started working here in 1958. I was seventeen. Mike's father, Henrich Mueller, built this inn when he returned from the war. He was quite an amazing man. His parents came from Bavaria. He was the hardest working, toughest son of a gun you'd ever meet. And he was a great leader."

"I'm sure he was. This is a pretty special place he built, and it seems his legacy lives on in his son. There's something extraordinary about it."

Walt sat back and looked intently at Jim for a moment, as if weighing something in his mind. He then leaned forward and said to Jim almost mysteriously, "You want to know the secret, don't you, son?"

Jim and Amanda both leaned forward instinctively. Jim lowered his voice and said, "So there is a secret! Then yes, Walt, I do want to know."

Walt gestured outward toward the dining room and lounge. "Look out there," he said. "Really look. What do you see?"

Jim's gaze followed the arc of Walt's sweeping gesture as he surveyed the dining room. "I see happy, relaxed guests enjoying a delicious breakfast."

"Okay. What else?" Walt prodded.

Jim looked from Walt back to the room. "Well, I see them all sort of enjoying each other's company, too. It's almost like everyone feels as though they belong right here."

"And?"

Jim said, "Um, well—I see the staff all providing great service. They treat every guest in the room as if they are the most important people here."

"Okay, that's a B-minus so far. Keep going," Walt pushed.

Jim looked slightly offended. "I don't know what you mean. What more is there? There are lots of guests enjoying a nice atmosphere, a great product, and great service. Isn't that it?"

"Not even close, son. Look beyond the surface. What you just described is the effect, not the cause. Look at Wendy and Rose and Melody. Look at Tanner, who's busing the tables. Look at Mike. Peek back there at Eva in the kitchen with her team. Watch them work. How would you describe it?"

Despite his growing frustration and his inclination to dismiss Walt as a doddering old fool, Jim did as he was told. He sat back and watched the staff for several minutes. He sipped his coffee and observed. While he did so, another server, not Wendy, delivered their food. She had beautiful long, curly auburn hair. She smiled at both of them and said, "Wendy's taking a big order and will be right back to check on you. I'm Rose. Is there anything you'd like right away?"

Jim and Amanda both shook their heads, and Walt said to her, "Thank you, my wild Irish Rose." She smiled shyly, patted Walt's shoulder, and moved on about her work.

As Jim watched them all, it was as if the background blurred in his vision. All he could see—with startling, sudden clarity—were the staff members. There was very little discussion between them. Occasionally, they would exchange glances, gestures, and smiles of appreciation and encouragement. He realized it was like watching ballet or a fantastic play in football—where each member's movements are in sync with all the others'. Whenever there was even a subtle change in one part of the room, they all adjusted seamlessly. It was as if delicate gossamer threads connected all of them. Jim felt a tingle like static electricity travel up his spine.

"It's all connected," Jim said aloud, not taking his eyes from the team.

A faint smile crossed Walt's face. "What do you mean by that? Connected by what?"

"They aren't just servers, a busboy, the kitchen, and a bartender. They're a team. They've somehow all linked together and formed a system. They're functioning as a unit."

"You're getting very close to A-plus territory now, Jim," Walt said. "What is it that allows them to link up like that, do you suppose?"

Jim said with growing excitement, "It's invisible, like energy. It's as if they have complete and total trust in one another. And Mike, though he's busy, too, is watching over them with total confidence—and they sense it, so they all rise to the occasion."

"*Vertrauen*," Walt said. "Heinrich used to call it *Vertrauen* in German. In English it means the energy of trust or faith. And it *IS* energy, Jim. It's all energy. You could say energy is everything."

Jim put down his fork and looked squarely at Walt. He repeated what Walt said, as if struggling to get his mind around it. He said aloud, but mostly to himself, "Energy is everything . . . The energy of trust is what makes a team. And trust starts with the leader." As he said those last words, he turned his head to look at Mike behind the bar. Mike, the living legacy of the great man who built the Gottschalk Inn. Mike, who reminded him of Milton Wallis.

Jim sat up bolt-straight in his chair. "Milt!" This was exactly what Milt had been trying to tell him all along. Jim's heart was pounding. He turned to Amanda, who was staring at him with a look bordering on concern.

She said, "Honey, are you all right? Your face is bright red." She touched his cheek with the back of her hand.

He looked at her and laughed out loud. Walt and Mary both looked amused and not the least bit surprised. He took her face in both his hands and planted a big kiss on her. "Oh, honey! I'm so much better than all right. I get it! Milt has been right all along! I'm the leader. It's all about the energy I bring to my team—all of them. Holy buckets! I get it!" He shook his head and covered his face with both hands, pressing his fingertips to his eyes. "It's so simple. How could I have missed it? My God, what have I been doing to my team?"

Walt reached over and placed his hand firmly on Jim's arm. "What matters most, son, is what you do *now*—and what you do moving forward. You can't do differently until you see differently. It sounds like maybe you should have a chat with this Milt character."

Jim looked at Walt with amazement and appreciation. "How can I ever thank you? Who *are* you?"

"I'm just an old fool who's spent a lot of time at the Gottschalk Inn. This place has heart. Always has. And I love it here."

"Well, I may still have a lot to learn, but I can state with authority that you are no fool. You may have just saved my career," Jim said.

"In that case, I'll send you my bill on Monday," Walt said, laughing. "In the meantime, you should finish your breakfast before I finish it for you. Eva gets offended if her cooking goes to waste." And he bit into a piece of Jim's toast.

They finished breakfast and chatted about other things. Mary told the story of how she and Walt met a few years after they were both widowed. Amanda talked about Jack and Emma and how well they were doing and talked a bit about teaching and how much she had loved it. Jim asked Walt dozens of questions about snowmobiles and trails and the area in general.

When they were done, Wendy brought two checks. Jim reached over and took them both. Walt protested at first, but Jim said, "Please. Please at least allow me to buy your breakfast. You can't imagine what you've done for me."

Walt removed his hand from the check folder and said, "Well, thank you, then. It's been a real pleasure to meet you. And best of luck to you at Wallis International."

Jim was surprised Walt remembered the name. None of Wallis's hotel brands bore the name of the parent company. He said, "Are you familiar with Wallis?"

Walt smiled, shrugged, and said, "I've heard of it."

As they left the restaurant, Jim made a point to stop at the bar. The breakfast crowd was thinning out, and Jim could see snowmobilers heading off in various directions across the lake. He said to Mike, "Hey, I know it's Saturday and you're busy, but any chance you'd have some time to talk later this afternoon? I have some ideas I'd like to share with you."

Mike said, "Why don't you come in around three, before we open the room for dinner? We'll have a scotch."

"That sounds fantastic. Thank you! I'll see you at three."

After Jim and Amanda returned to their room, he said, "I have to make a phone call. I can't wait to talk to Milt."

He was so full of energy and excitement, his hand shook as he dialed Milton Wallis's cell phone number. When Milt answered, Jim collected himself and said, "Milt. It's Jim Watts. I hope you and Julia did okay in the storm."

"Jim! We're just fine. And how about you? Are you working today? The offices are closed until Monday."

"No, Milt. I'm not working. Amanda and I are actually in Wisconsin. We didn't make it all the way back to the city before the storm hit. We decided to stay the weekend at a little inn over here. Say, Milt, I know tomorrow is Sunday, but there's something I'd really like to talk to you about. Mandy and I will be driving back to Chicago in the morning. Is there any chance we could meet later in the day?"

"Well, Jim, that sounds important. Is everything okay?"

"Oh, yes! Truly. Everything is just fine. I'd just like to sit and chat with you for a while."

"Well, I'd rather not go to the office on Sunday. Why don't you and Amanda come out to the house around four, and we'll have an early dinner. We'd be delighted to see you both."

"That would be great. That will give Mandy and I a few hours at home to freshen up. I'd rather meet with you at the house than at the office, anyway. Thank you so much, Milt. We'll see you tomorrow."

"You're welcome, son. See you then. Bye." And Milt hung up.

Jim looked at Amanda with excitement and anticipation. He took out his notebook and showed her what he'd written so far. To it, he added the following words:

Trust & Teamwork

Amanda slid the notebook toward her and took Jim's pen. She wrote something on the page and passed it back to him. She had made two changes: First she put a different symbol between the words Jim had written, so it now read:

Trust = Teamwork

And below it, she wrote in her beautiful, perfect cursive:

Energy is Everything

THE HEART OF A MAN

After spending some time in the room, with Amanda reading her book by the fire and Jim making lots of notes about ideas to discuss with Milt, they decided to explore the grounds a bit before Jim's meeting with Mike. They could see from their window that all the walking paths and patios had been cleared. They put on their boots and warm clothes and made their way downstairs.

They'd learned by watching the Sled Dogs come and go earlier that there were side doors on the lower level of the inn that opened to a network of walking paths along the lakeside of the property. They walked to the end of the hallway, past the restaurant and lounge, and stepped outside into the afternoon sun.

It was a bright, cloudless day. The snow was beginning to melt, and they could see chunks of it occasionally falling from the laden branches of the pine trees along the property. It felt surprisingly mild for mid-January in southern Wisconsin. Jim and Amanda meandered along the walking paths that branched out from and around the inn. They enjoyed the fresh air and watched as snowmobilers zipped across the frozen lake.

They followed one path that led to a lovely terrace near the lakeshore. The snow had been cleared from the area, and even though the wooden rocking chairs had been put away for the season, Jim knew as soon as he stepped onto the circular flagstone terrace that this was the spot he'd seen on the desktop wallpaper Thursday night. He said, "There's a photo of this place in autumn on the computers in the business center. You should see what it looks like when the fire's going and all these trees are in full color. It's absolutely stunning."

"I can only imagine," Amanda replied. "It's a beautiful spot. Look how much of the lake you can see from here." As she spoke, she sat down on the wide stone wall that encased the now-dormant fire pit. Jim walked around and sat by her side.

He said, "Let's plan to come back here. I want to see what the lake looks like from this very spot in the spring, summer, and fall. I understand now what Adam said when we checked in. There is something about this place that makes you feel grounded."

Amanda just took his hand and rested her head on his shoulder. They sat quietly for what might have only been a few minutes—or half an hour. It was one of those unique moments when time seemed to be flying by and standing still all at once.

Jim looked around, wanting to take it all in. He was consciously imprinting the sights, sounds, and general feeling of this place to his memory. As he followed the curve of the terrace, he noticed what appeared to be a bronze plaque affixed to the stone wall encircling the area. It was caked with snow, but he could see the word *heart* plainly. His curiosity piqued, he got up and stood before the plaque. The lower part was completely plastered with snow, but with one brush of his gloved hand, he could read the entire quote at the top. It said: "If you truly want to know the heart of a man, examine the fruits of his labor." Below it, he could see a date. He brushed a little harder to clear the snow from the remainder of the plaque.

Jim stood with his eyes fixed on the plaque and felt the blood drain from his face. He suddenly felt a chill. He rubbed the plaque again, as if rubbing it would somehow change the words affixed in bronze before him. He felt for a moment as if his head would explode, and he closed his eyes and pinched the bridge of his nose.

Amanda, sensing something was wrong, turned to look his way. She said, "Honey, are you all right? What's wrong?"

Jim's head was spinning. He collected himself to say slowly and carefully, "Amanda, how did you say you heard about this place? Who told you about it?"

"I heard about it from Susan, who owns the salon I go to. You know her—Susan Lawson. Her son Zach is Milt's assistant. Why? Jim, what's wrong? You're scaring me." She got up and walked to him. He said nothing, but gestured toward the plaque. She read aloud:

"'If you truly want to know the heart of a man, examine the fruits of his labor.' June 23, 1992. In loving memory of Heinrich Mueller, who brought HEART to all he encountered. A gift from Milton and Julia Wallis."

She stepped backward and grabbed Jim's arm. "Oh my God, Jim."

Jim just shook his head in disbelief. His thoughts were spinning out of control.

Amanda said, "How could we be here all this time and not know? How is that even possible?"

He whispered, almost inaudibly, "Anything is possible at the Gottschalk Inn. . . ." He turned to her and felt the blood rushing back to his face. Now he was turning bright red as he said, "I need to go see Mike right now."

He strode off quickly, leaving Amanda there, staring at the plaque in disbelief.

It was nearly three according to the clock in the lounge. Mike was cleaning and restocking the bar supplies for the dinner service. He looked up as Jim stepped into the bar, red-faced with what appeared to be tears in his eyes.

"So, what was all this? Some kind of cruel joke?" Jim nearly shouted at Mike. "Think it's funny to watch me make a fool of myself?"

Mike smiled and looked serene, as always. He poured two scotches and stepped from behind the bar. "I was wondering how long it would take you to connect the dots. Let's sit and have a drink."

"I don't want to sit and have a drink! I want some goddamn answers, Mike. You've known since Thursday I worked for Milton Wallis, and you didn't tell me he was connected to this place? Now I see his name on a friggin' plaque on your terrace? You tricked me! Does he know I'm here?"

Mike took the two glasses and sat down at a table by the windows. He calmly said, "Listen, Jim, I'll tell you the whole story—I'll tell you over this beautiful glass of scotch. Sit down and catch your breath."

Grudgingly, Jim complied. He took his coat off, sat, and drained his scotch in one gulp. In an uncharacteristically uncouth manner, he wiped his mouth with the back of his hand. He sat back, closed his eyes, and took a long, deep breath. He felt the warmth of the drink radiate through his chest, down his limbs, and to his extremities. While he sat with his eyes closed, Mike got up and poured him a glass of water.

"I think you better switch to this now, Jim. You're going to want to remember this conversation," Mike said.

Jim exhaled as if deflating and said, "I'm sorry I yelled like that. A little bit ago, I was really feeling like I was onto something—like I was figuring some things out. But now I'm more confused than when I got here. I just can't believe you didn't tell me, Mike."

"Well, Jim, you didn't ask," Mike said.

Jim looked at him blankly.

"I told you I was familiar with Wallis. If you had asked how, I would have told you then. But once I understood your situation, I figured it would be best if you didn't know—at least for a day or two so you could enjoy your time here."

"Would you have told me before I left?"

"Why do you think I asked you to come back when the restaurant was closed?" Mike chuckled. "I didn't want to run the risk of you coldcocking me in front of my guests."

Jim looked at Mike squarely for a moment and wondered if punching Mike would make him feel any better. Just the thought made him start to laugh. He covered his eyes with his hand and just shook his head. "Okay, okay. So I didn't ask. Can you help me understand how on earth I wound up in this situation? I feel like I just stepped into an episode of *The Twilight Zone*."

"Well, I'm not sure I can help you with that. I got the feeling you didn't just stumble across this place. How did you find out about us?"

"I think I've figured out that part. Amanda's hairdresser, Susan Lawson, told her about this place, and Susan's son is Milt's assistant."

"Susan! Yes, I remember her! Her son gave her a weekend here as a Mother's Day gift last year. He must have asked Milt for a recommendation."

"What I really want to know, Mike, is why? Why did this odd set of circumstances seem to conspire to get me here just now? The timing of the storm, Amanda remembering Susan's suggestion—it all seems a bit uncanny."

"Well, I already told you I believe everything happens for a reason. You told me Thursday night you had a lot to learn. . . . You've been here two days. Have you learned anything?"

Jim felt his little leather-bound notebook through his shirt pocket. "Actually, yes. That's what I wanted to talk to you about. First, though, tell me how Milton Wallis is connected to this place."

"Milt worked here. He worked for my dad back in the early days, like Walt. In fact, he and Walter were quite the pair of pals. I'm surprised Walt didn't tell you this morning."

"I was wondering how Walt would have heard about Wallis International. He didn't say a word about knowing Milt! This *is* a conspiracy!" But Jim wasn't upset anymore. He was too eager to hear the story. "Go on . . ."

"Well, Walt's a funny guy. I'm sure he figured you'd work it out in due time. Anyway, according to Dad, Milt was pretty gifted. He seemed to have a knack for understanding both the technical side of the business and what the guests wanted. Milt's father was killed in Korea, so Milt and my dad kind of adopted each other, I think. I didn't come along until later. So Milt has always been like a much-older brother or an uncle to me. When Dad passed in '92, Milt and Julia built that beautiful terrace and fire ring by the lake in his honor. Taking this place over left me with some pretty big shoes to fill. I can't tell you how many times I've gone to Milt for advice, and he's always been there for me. He's an amazing man. And that's the story."

Jim strained his memory to think of some of the things Milt had said in those conversations when Jim was half-listening. One statement came to mind: "There is no greater blessing in life than finding a wise mentor." Jim now realized Milt was talking about Heinrich Mueller. Jim took his notebook out and laid it on the table between them. "I've been taking notes for the past two days, and I wanted to share them with you. Being here has given me a chance to see some things that you do unbelievably well—and to think about how I can bring some of that to the Wallis hotels."

"I'm all ears," Mike replied as he took a sip of his scotch and sat back in his chair.

"First, we met Adam . . . who appeared out of nowhere in the midst of a raging snowstorm to carry our bags. Here's this brilliant kid, in one of the best med schools in the country, who is so unassuming, gracious, and service minded. And all I could think is that kid has humility.

"Then I met you, Mike, and see this amazingly classy bar. And Amanda met Sam, who not only noticed she was upset, but also found out why and fixed it for us by bringing up that TV. Amanda and I thought two things that first night: first, there's a great energy to this place; and second, the execution is impeccable.

"The next morning, we met Wendy and saw how unbelievably well she handled that poor old guy whose brother is dying in Minnesota."

"Frank . . ." Mike interjected. "He's a great guy."

"Right, Frank. The way she managed to stay patient with him and look beyond how he was acting on the surface to understand what was really going on inside—it just showed an unbelievable awareness.

"Then there was our day on the trail, which so many of your people made special for us: Billy, with his sincerity and good humor; Sam, with her signature enthusiasm; and Eva, who sent us love through a sandwich. It made me realize every person here is focused on building and maintaining relationships. And not just building relationships with us—that you can read in Guest Service 101—but with each other. That's what makes your guests want to keep coming back here—to be part of your family.

"And finally, I now realize my time with Walt this morning was a coaching session. He made me see that without genuine trust, there is no real teamwork. And there is a subtle but very real and very powerful difference. Which is why your restaurant staff can move around a packed room and make it look effortless—like a ballet."

Jim took a long drink of water while he caught his breath. He realized when he put his glass down Mike was grinning at him.

"Why are you looking at me all goofy like that? You think I'm crazy?"

"No, Jim. I don't think you're crazy at all. You just made my day."

"What do you mean?"

Mike reached into his pocket and took out his wallet. "Well, are you ready for one more strange coincidence?"

Jim raised his eyebrows and looked suspiciously at Mike. "Oh God, what? Did my mother work here, too, or something?"

"No, nothing like that. Have you noticed we have a lot a signs and sayings on our walls here?"

"Yes."

"What do almost all of them have in common?"

"Well, they all say stuff about love. Well, not really love, I suppose, but *heart*. Why?"

Mike removed a small plastic card from his wallet and placed it on the table in front of Jim, right next to Jim's notebook. It had the logo of the Gottschalk Inn at the top and said:

*At the Gottschalk Inn, we live our purpose by serving with **HEART:***

Humility

Energy x Execution

Awareness

Relationships

Trust = Teamwork

Jim stared at the card, dumbfounded. "That's impossible . . ."

Mike raised his eyebrows and cocked his head to one side. "After all this, you're still saying that?"

Jim looked at Mike and started laughing. Not just chuckling, but full-on belly laughing, guffawing, and snorting. He said as the tears rolled down his cheeks, "That's nuts! Come on, Mike, even you have to admit that is amazing!"

Mike started laughing, too. After a few minutes, they both settled down enough to speak. Mike said, "It is amazing. It's extraordinary because it proves something your boss, my mentor, told me a while back that I didn't fully believe."

"And what was that?"

"Milt told me, 'When you're living your mission, your purpose, you don't have to tell people what it is. They'll see it. And more importantly, they'll feel it.' I didn't completely believe that until right now. So, Jim, apparently you weren't just here to learn something. You were here to teach something, too."

Jim looked back and forth from his notebook to Mike's card. He was astounded. It was nearly identical. He noticed one small difference. "Mike, why is there a multiplication symbol between the words *Energy* and *Execution?*"

"Because that's exactly what they do to one another. They multiply. Look at it this way: On a scale of one to ten, if you're doing all the right things mechanically but with no heart, you could say you score a ten on execution, but maybe only a three on the energy side of the equation. Multiply them. That's a thirty. That's a failing grade—even though your execution is flawless. The opposite is also true. You can have the nicest, most loving people in the world on your team, but if the food tastes bad or the sheets are stained, you'll still come up with a failing grade because of poor execution. You've got to do both—and do both well."

Jim heard in an instant dozens and dozens of conversations with Milt replay in his head. His eyes brightened, and he suddenly took on a look of joyful anticipation, like a child on Christmas Eve. He looked at Mike and said, "I can't wait to talk to Milt!"

THE LEGACY

Jim and Amanda were up and packed early Sunday. They enjoyed one more great breakfast at the Gottschalk Inn and then said their thank-yous and goodbyes to their new friends. Jim and Mike shook hands and then embraced like brothers. Mike clapped Jim on the back and said, "Tell Milt hello for me. And go make us proud! You've got this."

As Jim and Amanda curved their way down the drive to leave the inn, Jim glanced over his shoulder for one last look at the wood-and-stone lodge that had looked so ungainly to him Thursday night. Now he saw a thing of beauty. Now he could see the fruits of Heinrich Mueller's labor. He saw the wide stone chimney, built by Billy's grandfather. He could imagine Milton Wallis here as a young man, impressing Heinrich, his future mentor, and falling in love with the business of hospitality. He could imagine all the lives touched and all the lives changed by this magical little place in the woods of Wisconsin.

He turned to Amanda, who looked radiant and relaxed, and said, "That was a good suggestion, honey. Maybe you should go into the hospitality business."

She smiled at him and said, "Thank you, dear. I'm thinking maybe I'd be a good travel agent."

He was a bit puzzled when he replied, "I'm sure you would, but why do you say that?"

She grinned at him and said, "Well, I got started by booking reservations for us at this great little inn in Wisconsin for April, July, and October."

He squeezed her hand and smiled.

The drive back to Chicago was an easy one. Though the evidence of the storm was everywhere, the roads were clear and dry. They chatted happily about all kinds of things but seemed to avoid talking about their upcoming dinner with Milt and Julia.

As the downtown Chicago skyline came into view, Amanda looked at Jim and asked, "Are you nervous about meeting with Milt?"

Jim said, "Not really nervous—there's just something I can't figure out. It's bothering me."

"What is it? What's bothering you?"

"If Milt has been so involved with the Gottschalk Inn all these years, if he's had the answers all along, why didn't he just tell me? He's been helping Mike. Why not help me?"

Amanda looked over at him and was filled with compassion. "Well, honey, I think you should ask him tonight."

Jim pressed the doorbell at Milt's home promptly at four o'clock. Considering Milton Wallis had made millions from Wallis International, his and Julia's home was fairly modest.

They had a beautifully renovated craftsman-style home. Julia answered the door and welcomed them inside. "Well, hello there! I'm so delighted to see you both. Please come inside." She hugged them both.

Jim felt funny handing his coat to his boss's wife, but Milt and Julia didn't believe in hiring people to do what you could do for yourself—although they could have easily afforded a full-time maid, if they wanted. At seventy, Julia was spry and energetic.

"Milton is just putting the finishing touches on dinner. He still loves to be in the kitchen, my Milt. He's making us a lovely beef tenderloin."

Jim's stomach growled. "It smells fantastic."

"Well, come in and sit. Can I pour you a drink? Maybe a glass of wine?"

"I'd love a glass of scotch," Jim said.

"And I'm always up for a glass of wine," Amanda said. "Oh, that reminds me! We had a few hours to relax at the house, and we brought you a little something from Jim's cellar." She handed Julia a bottle of very nice Cabernet Sauvignon from their wine collection at home.

"Well, thank you. That's just lovely. I'll set it in a nice, cool spot, and we'll have it with dinner."

Jim and Amanda were settled in the living room, enjoying their drinks and chatting with Julia about the storm, when Milt entered with a tray of cheese and crackers and crudités. "Welcome to *chez* Milton! How about a little something to take the edge off your hunger?"

Jim was honored to be served by his boss. He gladly enjoyed some snacks and sipped his glass of scotch. He looked over at Milt and suddenly felt a little nervous.

Milt noticed it and said, "You know, if you ladies will pardon us for a few minutes, I think Jim and I will head downstairs to the shop so I can show him what I've been working on. Jim, let's top off these beverages, and I'll show you what Julia calls 'man heaven.'"

Jim followed Milt down a set of cellar stairs into a very well-equipped woodshop. Jim said, "Wow, Milt, I had no idea you had so many talents outside of business."

Milt said, "Well, Jim, I think maybe you and I should spend a little more time together outside of the office."

"I'd like that, Milt. I realized I've worked for you a very long time, yet there's still a lot about you I don't know."

"Son, I heard the urgency in your voice yesterday, and I can tell you're anxious now. What was it you wanted to discuss?"

Jim set down his scotch on the workbench and took out his wallet. He removed the little plastic card Mike had given him and handed it to Milt.

Milt took the card and ran his fingers over it almost lovingly. "Ah . . . I see. You've had a bit of a history lesson, then?"

Jim said, "Milt, I haven't just had a history lesson, although that was certainly surprising. I've had a future lesson—the future of Wallis International Group."

Milt smiled and looked intently at Jim. "Tell me what you mean by that, Jim."

"That quirky little wayside rest in Wisconsin sets the absolute standard for what the hospitality industry is all about. I want to bring the magic of the Gottschalk Inn to Wallis. I don't want to just be in the business of providing hospitality. I want to provide hospitality from the HEART."

Milt's eyes began to get moist. "I knew you were the one."

"Milt, it was the craziest thing. I was taking all these notes while we were there, jotting down these one- and two-word entries to summarize the service. And the words I wrote are the very same words right here on this card! I still can hardly believe it."

"Well, at the Gottschalk Inn, they've become experts at living their purpose, their mission. And when you do that, people will see it. You don't have to tell them."

"Yeah, Mike says he believes that now, by the way. And he says hello." At this, Jim looked around Milt's shop. There were wooden toys and pieces of furniture, and then he noticed a painted sign on the wall that said: "Trust your heart, as it always speaks the truth."

"They've got signs just like that all over the Gottschalk Inn."

"I know," Milt said. "I made them."

Jim looked at Milt and held up the little card. He pointed to it and said, "So this is you? And the sayings on the signs, they're all you?"

"No, Jim. The wisdom isn't from me. It was entrusted to me to be passed on, as it will now be entrusted to you." Milt turned and opened a small filing cabinet that seemed to contain mostly templates and plans for woodworking projects. He removed a folder and carefully set it on the workbench. He turned on the light above the bench and opened the folder. He gently ran his fingertips over the yellowed sheet of paper that appeared to be thin and delicate, like the wings of a moth. He turned the paper toward Jim and gestured for him to read it.

April 26, 1971

My dear boy Milton,

So, how is life in the big city? We still miss you here at the inn. Poor Walter is like a lost dog without you. I have to double his work to keep his mind busy!

I got your letter about your struggles with the new hotel. I'm just an old Bavarian fool, but you've asked for my advice, so I will give it. I will share with you everything I know about true service—what was passed to me by my father.

I have two conditions, Milton, upon sharing this knowledge. First, you must agree to share this wisdom with my son Michael. He is still a boy but someday will become a man and will run my beloved Gottschalk Inn. I may be too old or gone by the time he is ready, so you must consent to do this for me. The second condition is that you must only share this knowledge when Michael, and the person you choose to succeed you in your business, is ready to receive it. I cannot tell you when that will be, only that there will be a sign and you will know when the time is right.

Milton, you are a bright young man. What a mind you have! With your brains, you will always do well in life. If you want your life, however, to be extraordinary, you must learn to listen to your heart as well. Trust your heart, Milton, for it always speaks the truth. When you do so, you will find that you will always know the right course of action. This business of innkeeping relies upon our ability to speak directly to the hearts of others. And to speak to the heart of man, you must speak from your own.

As you gain success—which you will, Milton—maintain a sense of humility. Remember this wisdom is for you, but not from you. Give more praise than you accept for yourself, and you will find yourself surrounded by loyalty.

Remember that the execution of our business is only half the battle. If we execute flawlessly in our daily work, but do so without the love and energy of service, we fail. And if we have the most genuine energy and spirit of service and take no action upon it, we fail. You must do both and embrace both fully.

Teach those who will be lucky enough to work for you to maintain a constant awareness of their surroundings and your guests. Not just an awareness of what occurs on the surface, but an awareness of the secret self of others— what drives their actions and their needs. Everyone has a story; awareness allows us to read it.

Everything you do every day for the rest of your life will depend upon the quality of the relationships you build with others, Milton. Teach your workers first to build strong, respectful bonds with each other, and the relationships with your guests will seem to flow outward effortlessly. Your customers will want to be in a place where the workers convey a sense of pride and belonging.

Remember *Vertrauen*. This is German for what in English you would call trust and faith. Work every day to earn the trust of your people and create an atmosphere that encourages them to trust one another. When you do those things, your individual workers will begin to function as a team.

Milton, think every day about the legacy you want to leave behind. If you truly want to know the heart of a man, examine the fruits of his labor. Work is good, Milton, when it produces good. Build your company not with the next ten years in mind, but with the next hundred years.

I am proud of you and the man you have become. I know, Milton, you will achieve great things. I may not be your true father, but I love you, my boy, as a true son.

With *Herz* (Heart),
Heinrich Mueller
Gottschalk Inn, 1971

Jim looked hurt. "I don't understand, Milt. If you knew the answers all along, why didn't you just tell me? I know it's no secret at Wallis that I've been floundering."

"There's an old Buddhist saying that goes, 'When the student is ready, the teacher appears.' You weren't ready."

"How do you know I wasn't ready?"

"Because every time I started talking to you about HEART, you sent me to talk to someone else. But this . . ." He picked up the little card from the Gottschalk Inn. "Signs don't get much clearer than this."

Jim blushed. He thought of all the times he intentionally directed Milt to his director of guest services. "I'm sorry, Milt. I truly am. But would you have let me fail?"

"You wouldn't have failed. To quote my beloved mentor, 'With your brains, you will always do well in life.' I was just waiting for you to start listening to your heart. Some lessons in life can't be taught with words alone. The wisdom of HEART must be experienced to be learned. I could have read you this very same letter a week ago, and you'd have thought me a silly, sentimental old man. For you to truly understand, embrace, and then live the five principles of HEART, you must *feel* them—not just know them in your head. I have always believed in you, Jim. That's why I chose you to lead. You've had the answers all along. You had simply not fully connected with and trusted that inner voice that has been beckoning you to this place and moment in time. Now you can move forward and begin applying and teaching the principles of HEART to our organization."

"Milt, I have so many ideas of how to bring HEART back to Wallis International Group. I can hardly wait to share them with you."

"Well, good. I can hardly wait to hear them."

Jim perched himself on the little stool by Milt's workbench and cleared his throat. "Okay, so the first thing I was thinking about is—"

Milton put up his hand and interrupted Jim. "I can hardly wait to hear them—first thing Monday morning at the office. Right now, we've got two beautiful women, an expertly prepared meal, and a very nice bottle of wine waiting for us upstairs."

Jim smiled at Milton Wallis—his mentor. "You are so right. Lead on!"

EPILOGUE

JIM WATTS
COO, WALLIS INTERNATIONAL GROUP
CHICAGO, ILLINOIS

So now you know my story—at least the part that tells how I came to learn and live the five principles of HEART. It's been a year now since I made that first terrifying presentation to the board. Milton, of course, was there to support me, and I was a little shocked at how many of the board members seemed to have been waiting for me to stand up and say exactly what I said.

Mike Mueller and all our friends at the Gottschalk Inn continue to inspire me. Mike and I have become close—we share a mentor, after all.

Amanda and I returned, as planned, to watch the seasons change at the Gottschalk Inn. The photo of Milt and Julia's terrace in fall didn't even come close to doing justice to the beauty of the lake and trees in autumn. Which is a good thing—because our daughter, Emma, will be getting married on that very terrace next September. Yes, my kids, Jack and Emma, love the Gottschalk Inn, too. Emma wants to write about it—and how to apply the principles of HEART to her counseling practice. Extraordinary.

If you're facing the same challenges Wallis International faced in building loyalty, consistently delivering extraordinary service, and keeping your employees engaged, begin applying the principles of HEART in your organization and just watch what happens. You will soon notice both employees and guests leaving your business feeling good and thinking, *That place is different.*

We are seeing remarkable results already. The Wallis employees had been starving for real connection. Now engagement scores are up and turnover is trending down. Our service scores have improved every single month since we've brought HEART back to the organization. What I find most extraordinary about our service survey results is that in addition to the numerical scores improving, we've seen a measurable increase in the number of guests who write comments and mention a Wallis employee by name. We are also seeing a gradual uptick in return guests. We're building loyalty.

So if you want to engage your employees, deliver extraordinary service, and create loyal guests, bring HEART to your organization and your team. Remember that the five principles of HEART must be applied and lived to be truly understood.

And just like the Gottschalk Inn and now Wallis International, when you bring HEART to your organization, anything is possible.

This wisdom has now been entrusted to you, as it was entrusted to me. Use it well and seek opportunities to pass it on.

You are ready.

PART II

YOUR STORY

FROM FICTION TO HOSPITALITY FROM THE HEART REALITY

Yes, Jim Watts and the Gottschalk Inn are fictional and ideal, while your business exists, strives, struggles, and perhaps sometimes bleeds in reality. So you may be thinking, *Well, that's all nice, but how can I possibly create any of that in my organization?* Or, *That's all well and good, but I barely have time to get through my emails; how am I supposed to find time to connect with people?*

In this section of *Hospitality from the HEART*, we'll answer those questions, give you some very practical ways to evaluate how your organization is performing now in regards to each of the five principles, and offer you action steps to bring HEART to life in your everyday work. Use these questions as a framework to create meaningful discussions with your organizational leaders and with your team. Adapt them in ways that make sense for your business. Think of them as a buffet: take and use what resonates with you, and leave what doesn't. Listen to your heart, for it always speaks the truth. We have found that, without fail, employees support what they help create.

The subtitle of this book makes three promises. We state that creating a Hospitality from the HEART culture will help you:

- Engage your employees

- Deliver extraordinary service

- Create loyal guests

These three promises are the ultimate trifecta of successful hospitality organizations. They appear to be separate, but they are, in fact, inseparable. You cannot deliver extraordinary service and create loyal guests without highly engaged employees. And it all starts with people like Adam, Sam, Wendy, and Eva at the Gottschalk Inn—those who make the beds, fix the sinks, set the tables, and book the reservations. It begins with engagement.

Gallup studies on employee engagement show that as few as 28 percent of employees are fully engaged and have the opportunity to work at their full potential daily. That leaves a staggering 72 percent of all teams, yours included, working at less than their full potential—not being inspired, developed, and deployed to give their best to the team. This creates an epidemic of lost productivity. Even if that 72 percent of less-than-engaged employees are average performers and you can still achieve 90 percent guest satisfaction, it's the 10 percent of dissatisfied guests who are your greatest opportunity—greatest opportunity to build loyalty and thus increase profitability. So what's that 10 percent worth to you? If you're a million-dollar-per-year business, that's $100,000 in lost revenue. If you're one of the big boys and you're turning $5 million a year, that's a half-million dollars that just walked out the door. And if you're the mom-and-pop ice-cream shop that fights to get a half million in revenue per year, 10 percent costs you $50,000—that's your rent, or worse, your business. By the way, none of that includes the marketing costs of finding new guests to replace the ones you've lost.

In Daniel Pink's groundbreaking book on motivation, *Drive: The Surprising Truth About What Motivates Us,* he identifies three key factors that must exist for optimum motivation. They are the cornerstone of engagement, and they will naturally emerge in organizations that have HEART.

The first of Pink's three factors is *autonomy.* People want the freedom to work without being micromanaged. Set the boundaries, give direction, and then get out of the way. Train them to be experts, and then allow them to show their expertise; allow them to shine.

The second factor is *mastery.* Human beings are amazingly resilient. We're downright stretchy. And we thrive when we are given challenges that require us to struggle a bit, to learn, and to grow. It worked for Jim Watts, right? Give your team the questions, then resist the temptation to give them the answers. You're the leader because someone allowed *you* to learn. Do the same for your employees.

The third factor, which is supremely important in creating a HEART-centered culture, is *purpose.* The "why" your business exists is so much more important than the "how" or the "what." All people want to feel they are a part of something larger than themselves and know their work is important. When your mission is clear and inspires your team to truly feel the HEART of the organization, it allows them to connect to that purpose and, perhaps more importantly, show that vision to your guests through their everyday work.

What's important to understand about HEART—Humility, Energy x Execution, Awareness, Relationships, and Trust = Teamwork—is that this is not another "program." It is not so much about anything you *do* as it is about *who you are*. Living and working with HEART doesn't require a big rollout. You don't need a single banner or a slick campaign. You just have to begin every day with a renewed commitment to the HEART principles and with a willingness, like that of Heinrich Mueller and Milton Wallis, to both learn and teach. Just like at the Gottschalk Inn, anything is possible at your organization, too.

YOU, Leading from the **HEART**

Engaged Employees

Loyal Guests

BUSINESS SUCCESS

Extraordinary Service

HUMILITY

The first principle of HEART Jim Watts realized was Humility. In this quote, C. S. Lewis captures the essence of how we define humility as a principle: "True humility is not thinking less of yourself; it is thinking of yourself less."

Humility is not often a valued commodity in the business world, so putting it into action may not seem natural at first. One way to start thinking about humility is to ask yourself the following:

- Do I provide service from the mindset that our company exists only because our guests do?

- And do I, as a leader, treat my employees as more important to the company and to our mission than I am myself?

- Finally, do I ask for help from others, even when doing so reveals I don't have all the answers?

Only when you can truly answer yes to all three questions are you living the principle of humility. John C. Maxwell, bestselling author, noted speaker, and pastor who has published more than sixty books focusing primarily on leadership, said, "People don't care how much you know, until they know how much you care."

Here's a true story Brandon experienced early in his career that addresses this concept:

> *As a young up-and-coming general manager in the rapidly growing Famous Dave's BBQ organization, Brandon was eager to leave his mark and to share his knowledge with others. He was leading a meeting with his management team and spoke up frequently in an effort to help the team, offer advice, and share his insights. Though he didn't know why, he noticed at some point the energy in the room shifted and the meeting became much less productive. After the meeting, Brandon asked if he could chat with the kitchen manager about the shift in energy during the meeting. When Brandon asked him what was wrong, the kitchen manager replied with a question: "Brandon, am I the kitchen manager?" Brandon replied yes. And then the kitchen manager responded with the statement that would change how Brandon led his people. He said, "Then let me be the kitchen manager." Brandon was abashed. He learned that day that having all the answers is not what earns you the respect of others. What truly earns a leader respect is allowing others to grapple with challenges and find the answers themselves. Though it sounds ironic, what makes a leader truly great is humility.*

So what can you do to have and demonstrate humility and encourage your leaders and developing team to show it as well?

DISCUSSION QUESTIONS

Questions to Ask Yourself

How has being in the hospitality/service industry helped me grow as a person?

How does it feel when I am around/work with a "know-it-all" person?

How does it feel when I am around/work with someone who has a sense of openness?

What are the key characteristics of people whom I admire in the business world? Why are those characteristics important?

What is the value in having a mentor?

To whom in my life could I reach out and ask if he/she would be a mentor on my Hospitality from the HEART journey?

Whom are the people in my life I could mentor?

What are my strengths?

What are my opportunities for growth and improvement?

Am I building a strong team by surrounding myself with people who complement my strengths and opportunities for growth?

Questions to Ask Your Leadership Team

What are our strengths and opportunities individually and collectively?

Are we doing an extraordinary job of creating a culture of humility, growth, and development within our organization? Why or why not?

How will we be role models in encouraging our team members to ask for help and guidance when it is needed?

What structure(s) must we put in place within our organization to ensure the continued growth and development of our teams?

How are we currently doing with obtaining feedback from our guests?

How are we currently doing with obtaining feedback from our staff/team?

What must we do to improve our ability to embrace, discuss, and implement any needed changes based on the feedback we receive?

What are the successful organizations in this world? What makes them successful? How do we compare with them in those areas?

Questions to Ask Your Staff/Team

Why is it important to be confident in our delivery of Hospitality from the HEART and also be open to feedback on ways we can improve?

What does it feel like when you work with a "know-it-all"?

Why is it important for our team to come from a place of love and service?

Why is it important for us to continue to grow and learn on a daily basis?

What benefits, personally and professionally, do you gain individually from your commitment to growth and development?

What benefits does the team and organization gain from your individual commitment to growth and development?

How does it benefit you or the organization when the leadership team demonstrates humility?

ACTION STEPS

- Get to know your team and your guests:

- Ask questions, take notes, take the time to really get to know the people you are serving—including those on your team.

- Ask your team and your guests for feedback—good and bad. There is always something to learn and opportunities to get better when you have an open mind and open heart.

- Remember to be flexible. It's important to have a plan, and it's just as important to know when the plan needs to be adjusted.

- Use the resources all around you, including your people. Ask for help when you need it, and give the opportunity to your team to feel the sense of pride to come up with solutions and make things happen.

- We, as humans, follow the laws of nature, which state that you are either growing or dying. Commit to grow and learn on a daily basis; be open to seeing things differently and appreciate everyone's input and ideas.

- Remember that everything that feels new to you now will eventually feel natural—with practice and patience.

- Study the best of the best. Do not study the average. You will become what you study.

- Become an expert in your business by learning, growing, and choosing mentors to help keep you grounded, inspired, and guided.

- Stay away from the three most dangerous words: "I know that."

- Keep in mind no one wants to be around "I know that"–type people.

- Remember that we don't have all the answers, and people don't expect us to.

ENERGY × EXECUTION

The second principle of HEART Jim Wallis learned is Energy x Execution. That's right: "x" as in "times," as in multiplication. So often in business, we focus solely on the execution—the scripts, the steps, the policies and practices, and the rules. Have you ever walked into a retail store that had door greeters? These are people whose primary job is to welcome you. But we bet you've met more than one greeter who just sort of looked past you and said robotically, "Hi . . . welcome to XYZ-Mart" with such a lack of enthusiasm, it felt more like being kicked in the shin than greeted. Yeah, they followed the script, and yet something is clearly missing from those exchanges. What is it? Energy. Energy is *everything*!

Energy is contagious and impacts those around us. It is who you are and how you show up at work, at home, and within society. Energy is a state of being, or the attitude you have within any situation, regardless of circumstances. Energy is living with passion and confidence and being solution conscious. Energy is the effort and commitment you choose to put forth. Energy is how you make people feel.

Execution is acting or doing. It is having goals and objectives. Execution is getting the job done and raising your level of competency in your role. Execution is following through until the end and digging deeper within yourself and those around you in order to accomplish the necessary results.

And what is the product of this equation of Energy x Execution? When you multiply your standard of energy and your standard of execution, the product equals your results. Results are the ends that inspire us to the next level personally and professionally. Results are created through the discovery of what we are capable of and how much we can impact every aspect of our personal and professional lives. Results are what drive businesses, teams, and people. Without results, we have nothing.

The scale we use to measure energy and execution is a 1 to 10 scale—10 being extraordinary, and 1 being awful.

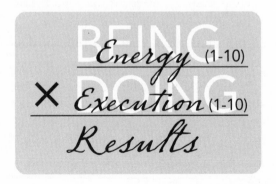

You can have the most beautiful rooms, the cleanest bathrooms, and the tastiest food, but if you're all execution with no energy (or the wrong energy!), you're failing. You're also failing if you have extraordinary energy, but are unable to execute.

Even if your team members score a 9 or 10 on execution, if they're only a 5 or 6 on energy, you're reaching *at best* 60 percent of your potential results. In what context is 60 percent ever a passing grade? And will 60 percent bring that customer back to your business, time and time again?

We use the formula of Energy x Execution = Results to categorize any guest-service experience at one of five levels:

5 LEVELS OF **RESULTS**

5	**Extraordinary**	*(90-100)*
4	Great	*(70-89)*
3	Good 'nuff	*(40-69)*
2	Transactional	*(20-39)*
1	Awful	*(1-19)*

Based off of ratings of Energy (1-10) x Execution (1-10)

Have you been settling for "good 'nuff" service? In this competitive market, industry, and world, is anything less than extraordinary really going to get you where you need to be? Will it make guests really notice the difference between you and your competitor?

The number one factor in the success of your business is your employee behaviors. So take a very serious look at your organization. What are your standards? Don't just pull out that dusty file of service standards in the filing cabinet. What are your standards *in practice*?

Other businesses can duplicate what you do and how you do it (your execution), but they can never duplicate why you do it—your purpose—and the way you make your guests and team *feel* while doing it (your energy). Energy is memorable and is a choice. We'll say it again, because it's worth repeating: Energy is everything!

Life is an echo. The energy you put out into the world comes back. If you send positive energy, love, and genuine caring out to the guests and team members, you will get the same in return, just as those working at the Gottschalk Inn did.

Energy x Execution. Without both factors at the 9–10 level, your results and your business will never be extraordinary. So how do you get there?

DISCUSSION QUESTIONS

Questions to Ask Yourself

On a scale of 1 to 10, what is my current rating for the level of energy I have been bringing to my job and organization?

On a scale of 1 to 10, what is my current rating for the level of execution I have been bringing to my job and organization?

What is my current level of results? (Energy x Execution)

What are my thoughts and feelings about my level of results?

I need to ask myself the Four Power Questions:

1. What is working for me?

2. What is not working for me?

3. What have I learned from this?

4. What will I do differently moving forward?

What are three things I will do to improve my level of energy?

What are three things I will do to improve my level of execution?

Questions to Ask Your Leadership Team

On a scale of 1 to 10, how would you currently rate our leadership team on our level of energy? Why?

On a scale of 1 to 10, how would you currently rate our leadership team on our level of execution? Why?

What is the current level of results (Energy x Execution) for our leadership team?

How would you currently rate your teams (departments) on their level of energy?

How would you currently rate your teams (departments) on their level of execution?

What is the current level of results (Energy x Execution) for your teams?

How would you currently rate our entire organization on its level of energy?

How would you currently rate our entire organization on its level of execution?

What is the current level of results (Energy x Execution) for our entire organization?

How will we teach this formula of Energy x Execution = Results to every member of our organization?

How will we ensure that this formula becomes part of our daily dialogue with our team members?

We need to ask ourselves the Four Power Questions:

1. What is working for us?

2. What is not working for us?

3. What have we learned from this?

4. What will we do differently moving forward?

Questions to Ask Your Staff/Team

What are some examples of extraordinary hospitality?

What are some examples of awful hospitality?

What are the standards (expected levels of energy and execution) that would make you proud to work for our organization?

On a scale from 1 to 10, what do you believe our current standards for energy are?

On a scale from 1 to 10, what do you believe our current standards for execution are?

What is our current level of results (Energy x Execution)? How does that make you feel?

We need to ask ourselves the Four Power Questions:

1. What is working for us?

2. What is not working for us?

3. What have we learned from this?

4. What will we do differently moving forward?

What are some examples of extraordinary energy?

What are some examples of awful energy?

What are some examples of extraordinary execution?

What are some examples of awful execution?

What are three things we will do to improve our level of energy?

What are three things we will do to improve our level of execution?

ACTION STEPS

- Use the formula of Energy x Execution = Results and the Four Power Questions on a daily basis to benchmark and measure your progress in building a Hospitality from the HEART culture.

- Hire and develop the best. Make a plan and act on it; learn and adapt accordingly. Keep moving forward.

- Be clear about the expectations and standards for your team, and then give members the tools, resources, and autonomy to make the standards happen. Coach and train where needed, but let your team do their jobs. *You will get exactly what you accept.*

- Be consistent and passionate about why you are in business—always creating, speaking, and developing the Hospitality from the HEART culture.

- Focus on and reward what your team is doing well or right, and it will reinforce the desired behaviors. *You get what you focus on.* Correct and retrain the other behaviors.

  - Consider some unfortunate realities of many managers and leaders:

    - We recognize team members 100 percent of the time when they do something wrong.

    - We recognize team members 1 percent of the time when they do something right.

- If someone is incapable of being a 9 or 10 in energy and execution in a particular role, find them a different role. They deserve an opportunity to do what they do best and what they are passionate about. And your guests deserve to have people serving them who are experts and passionate about serving them at an extraordinary level.

- Build your people, and they will build your results.

  - Keep in mind research conducted by Marcial Losada on feedback that shows we must have a 3-to-1 ratio of positive-to-negative feedback in order to create a culture of performance. If you fall below that standard, you will negatively impact the entire business. Losada's research also shows that the highest-performing teams and leaders have created a culture with a 6-to-1 ratio of positive-to-negative feedback.

- Hold your leaders to a high standard of both energy and execution. Add it to your performance evaluations, and use the formula as a tool for periodic self, team, and organizational evaluations.

- Remember that if you have an energy challenge in your business, you have a leadership challenge in your business. Maya Angelou once wrote:

> *"People will forget what you said.*
> *People will forget what you did.*
> *But people will never forget how you made them feel."*

AWARENESS

Now on to the third principle of HEART: Awareness. The emerging field of social neuroscience proves that awareness is not something that can be faked. We, as humans, are designed with highly sensitive receptors in our brains, called spindle cells, that allow us to "tune in" with amazing speed and accuracy to the social situation around us. Yes, there is real science behind how we connect with one another. These cells literally allow us to sync up with other people instantaneously, and they connect us much like multiple devices sharing a Wi-Fi network. This state of being in sync provides us with a wealth of information about the needs, intentions, and emotional states of others—particularly if we learn to focus on it.

This neural Wi-Fi also creates what scientists call "emotional contagion" in groups and organizations. Emotional contagion is exactly what it sounds like—the most powerful emotion in the group spreads, like the flu, and eventually "infects" the majority or the entire group. If you've ever worked on a team riddled with complaining and negativity, you know this feels a lot like being sick. Emotional contagion can work to your advantage, though—if you strategically and systemically "inoculate" your team against negativity by being genuinely positive yourself and by supporting positive behaviors and people in your organization.

Everyone has a story; every guest who walks through the lobby doors has a tale to tell. Awareness allows you to "read" that story and respond accordingly—whether the story is "I've had a horrible day, and I don't want to talk; I just want my room," or "I've had a horrible day, and I could really use a little cheerful interaction."

Mere *satisfaction* for our guests does not build guest loyalty—they can get satisfaction anywhere. We must use awareness to create an extraordinary experience (with both energy and execution) in order to make our guests feel important and connected to us. By tuning in like the characters who worked at the Gottschalk Inn did, we too can show guests what real hospitality is.

So how do you build a team of highly aware individuals who are attuned to one another and to the needs of your guests?

DISCUSSION QUESTIONS

Questions to Ask Yourself

What are some concrete ways to define "being fully present" to my employees and guests?

How does being fully present impact my interactions with the guests?

On a scale of 1 to 10, how present am I when I am doing my job?

How does raising my level of awareness allow me to deliver Hospitality from the HEART at a higher level?

How often do I follow my heart/intuition to make decisions that will serve our guests and organization?

Do I take initiative to make things happen that would benefit our guests and organization? Why or why not?

How do I communicate with other team members about what I am seeing and feeling on a daily basis to help us improve as an organization?

How many senses do I activate and pay attention to when I am in the workplace?

Questions to Ask Your Leadership Team

As a leadership team, how aware are we of what our guests truly need and want?

As a leadership team, how aware are we of what our teams truly need to grow and develop into fully engaged employees?

Does our organization have too many rules and policies that restrict our team/staff from being able to best serve our guests?

How often are we visiting with our teams/staff—taking them on an "awareness walk" around the property, asking questions, getting their insights, sharing our observations and insights, and discussing new possibilities of how we can better serve our guests and organization?

How do we incorporate the "awareness walk" within our organization—encouraging the use of the five senses (sight, smell, touch, taste, and hearing)—and how can we have it become part of our daily routine?

What will the process be within our organization for adapting new ways of doing things when we discover they provide a higher level of service to our guests?

What will we do on a daily basis to ensure our team members know that their presence, passion, and performance are critical to our success?

How do we ensure our staff is aware of community businesses, activities, and happenings to prepare them to exceed guest expectations when questions arise related to the community in which we do business?

Questions to Ask Your Staff/Team

On a scale of 1 to 10, how empowered do you feel to take initiative, the way the characters of Adam, Wendy, and Sam do, to serve our guests at the extraordinary level?

What more can we do as an organization to identify and remove obstacles that prevent you from doing your job at the highest of levels?

How can we be better attuned to our guests and better able to serve them?

What opportunities have we missed to create better financial performance within our organization?

What obstacles within our organization do we seem unaware of that have actually hindered us from providing extraordinary service to our guests?

How do we best adapt those obstacles in order to serve our guests *and* maintain our financial performance?

ACTION STEPS

- Challenge your team/staff to each submit one way that your business can better serve your guests, improve operations, and/or increase financial performance every month. Use those suggestions to improve your own awareness of your organization.

- Be present. The only thing you and your team control is the present moment. Have a vision of the future, learn from the past, but focus your team and energy on the present to create extraordinary experiences for every single guest—one heart at a time.

- Spend time getting to know your team and your guests. Challenge yourself to really know, understand, and appreciate them—recognize them. Remind yourself to stay in the moment when you're interacting with others. The investment of time and energy will make them *feel* more valued and appreciated, thus they will *feel* more connected with you and your business.

- Silence your phone and put it face down when you're interacting with someone. How do you feel when you're talking with people and they keep looking at their phones?

- Your perspective, how you see the world, affects everything you do. So when you scan or "see" the world, do you see a world of possibilities? Or do you see what's wrong with the world? Your perspective dictates everything else. Look for possibilities, opportunities, and interesting puzzles to solve. Don't settle for the status quo.

- Teach your team to use trust, intuition, and feeling to sense when something is good and when something is amiss. Pay attention to the smallest of details and hints.

- Train your organizational leaders in the science of emotional and social intelligence.

- Use all of your senses—sight, smell, hearing, taste, and touch—to *feel* your business.

- Hire positive people and allow the principle of emotional contagion to go to work for you. They will "infect" the team. They have the natural talent to build extraordinary relationships with others.

- Incorporate the awareness walk into your operations immediately. Before, during, and after shifts, encourage your team/staff to continuously keep all five senses on full alert and be ready to take action to better serve your guests and organization.

- Celebrate both your successes and your failures as learning opportunities by sharing them at your daily team/staff meetings. Make sure everyone is up to date and aware of how well the team is continuing to deliver Hospitality from the HEART.

RELATIONSHIPS

The fourth principle of Hospitality from the HEART is Relationships. Now, we recognize that this word has been thrown around carelessly in business for a long time, but we want you to really think in very specific terms about the kind of relationships you want to build with your guests and with your teams. We are social creatures. From the cradle to the grave, our lives are built upon a complex web of relationships with others. And science shows the quality of those relationships is tied directly to our health, happiness, and success—not just in business, but in life.

There's some very interesting new Harvard research on happiness. It can be summarized in one sentence:

Success does not lead to happiness;
happiness leads to success.

The relationships you build have to be real. People can smell emotional commitment a mile away. If you are not committed to an extraordinary guest experience or a culture of Hospitality from the HEART, everyone will *feel* it. As we stated earlier, competitors can never duplicate or steal the way you create long-term relationships and the way you make people *feel*. And once you get really good at it, competitors will drive themselves crazy, copying *what* you do and wondering why it doesn't get them the same results. Sounds fun, doesn't it?

Here is a brief story from coauthor Katherine's experience that addresses this truth:

> *Katherine once worked with a general manager of a large casino resort property who understood the importance of building relationships with team members and guests. He struggled, however, to find the time to talk with the employees out on the casino floor or in the restaurants or hotel. He was extremely driven and spent the vast majority of his time in meetings, answering emails and calls, or reviewing reports. Though he wanted to speak with people, he often found ten or twelve hours would pass with him barely ever leaving his office. He decided to hold himself accountable in a very unique way. He kept ten pennies in a little dish on his desk, and every morning, he would place those ten pennies in his left pocket. Every time he talked with, laughed with, or just engaged a team member or guest, he moved one of the pennies to his right pocket. He held himself accountable for making sure all ten pennies made it to the right pocket by the end of the day. Eventually, it became a habit, and he didn't need the pennies anymore. And the frontline employees on his team absolutely loved him. They felt he cared—and they showed that same level of caring to the guests.*

Contrary to popular belief about building a successful business, numbers don't drive people; rather, people and relationships drive numbers. Building meaningful relationships has a direct impact on your bottom line. One Gallup study estimates that US businesses lose $360 billion each year in lost productivity from employees who have poor relationships with their supervisors. Also according to Gallup, for employees to feel valued and committed to a workplace and to have a good relationship with their organization, they need to receive some form of recognition every seven days.

It's pretty obvious that building great relationships with your employees promotes engagement and reduces turnover. So that goes right to your bottom line as well. There's an important reality check here, though: as you build your Hospitality from the HEART culture and get progressively clearer about your expectations and standards for employee and guest relationships, it will also become clear who best fits that culture and who doesn't. You may have leadership moments ahead of you. It's okay to be selective about who becomes part of, and stays with, your organization. Making those decisions can set people free who don't embrace your standards, and perhaps they'll enjoy your culture more from the viewpoint of a guest. Jon Gordon, best-selling author and expert on building great cultures, says, "If you're working harder on your employees' success than they are, then you have to let them go."

So what can you do to really begin building the kind of relationships you want with your guests and team members?

DISCUSSION QUESTIONS

Questions to Ask Yourself

Do I do the best I can to build great relationships with my team members? Why or why not?

When was the last time I personally recognized a team member for his or her service to our guests and organization?

When was the last time I personally recognized a guest for his or her loyalty to our organization?

How well do I really know my team members?

What actions will I take to improve the quality of relationships with my team members?

How well do I really know our guests?

What actions will I take to improve the quality of my relationships with our guests?

Questions to Ask Your Leadership Team

On a scale of 1 to 10, how well does our culture demonstrate to our team/staff that we genuinely care about them as people and professionals?

How can we better demonstrate our care and appreciation for their service?

On a scale of 1 to 10, how well does our culture demonstrate to our guests that we genuinely care about them as people and customers?

How can we better demonstrate our care and appreciation for our guests' patronage?

What will it take to build meaningful relationships with our team members?

What will it take to build meaningful relationships with our guests?

What is the true value of a lifetime guest versus a one-time guest?

What is the true value of having an extraordinary team member who serves the organization for ten years versus one who leaves after a year?

Do we have the "right" people on our team in order to deliver our mission every day to our guests?

Would you want your kids working for this leadership team?

What will we do to ensure we are hiring, continuously growing, and developing the "right" people who fit our Hospitality from the HEART culture?

How do we create a healthy environment for our team to give us feedback?

Questions to Ask Your Staff/Team

On a scale of 1 to 10, how well do we create an atmosphere where we can build great relationships with our team members?

How can we improve on this?

On a scale of 1 to 10, how well does our culture create an atmosphere where we can build great relationships with our guests?

How can we improve on this?

What is the value of having extraordinary relationships within our organization?

What is the value of having extraordinary relationships with our guests?

Are you happier when you have strong relationships with team members and/or guests? Why?

ACTION STEPS

- Challenge yourself and your team to approach your guests and each other from a place of love and service. We can use as many business-y words as we like and say people want to feel "valued," "included," and "appreciated," but the fundamental truth is that human beings thrive on love.

- Take the time to visit with your team members. Find out their life stories. What are their goals and aspirations within the organization and beyond?

- Take the time to visit with your guests. What brings them to your business, and what keeps them coming back?

- Building extraordinary relationships is a daily discipline. Create and invest the time and energy to make it happen. Make engaging with, interacting with, and learning about your team members and guests a daily habit. Until it becomes a true habit, build it into your calendar.

- Focus on the lifetime value of your team and your guests. Treat them according to their true value—priceless! We tend to treat one-time guests differently for whatever reason, but why? Treat everyone as if they are VIPs, and see what happens to retention and loyalty—it will skyrocket!

- Create a culture where your business is a conduit to your team members' dreams. It will be a growth and learning experience for them to craft who they are and what they desire to be. Create an environment that rewards performance and impact and that celebrates new opportunities *earned* within the organization or even with a new organization—it's about the person becoming more.

- Every guest interaction is a moment of truth. It is a measurement of whether you are creating extraordinary relationships. Every thought, word, and action dictates whether you are living up to your standards. Make every phone call, webpage, menu, team interaction, décor choice, etc. a moment of truth that aligns your actions with your mission to create a Hospitality from the HEART culture.

- Genuinely thank guests and team members who bring issues to your attention. For every one guest that speaks up, there may be ten who remain silent but leave unhappy. Challenges and problems are really *huge* opportunities in disguise to win over both guests and team members. How you handle problems will dictate the relationship and level of trust (thus loyalty) both of those groups will have in your business.

TRUST = TEAMWORK

The fifth and last principle of HEART is Trust = Teamwork. Henry Ford, a real Hospitality from the HEART business-man, once said, "Trust people and they will be true to you. Treat them greatly and they will show themselves to be great." At the foundation of a true Hospitality from the HEART culture—and all great organizational cultures—is trust. Great leaders know it is their job to set expectations, to train, to coach, and then to allow people to do their jobs. The people who work for you want to know you believe in them and their abilities.

In the same vein, it is of the utmost importance that your employees trust the organization and trust their leaders to deliver the promises and commitments of the organization. Be very careful to ensure your words and your actions align. Be impeccable in your word. Employees will come to your organization ready to trust—to give you and your leadership team the benefit of the doubt. Once you've violated that sacred trust, however, it takes a major commitment of both time and energy to earn it back.

An integral part of building trust is communication. If you feel you're overcommunicating, then you might be getting *close* to communicating enough. If you don't make your culture, values, and standards completely clear, your employees will make them up on their own. Where there is a void in communication, that's where fear, doubt, and negativity will creep in to your culture—like viruses. This erodes trust and damages relationships.

Your guests want to feel a measure of trust as well. Once you've shown your guests true Hospitality from the HEART, they will come to expect it of you—they will trust in you to deliver the extraordinary experience again and again.

DISCUSSION QUESTIONS

Questions to Ask Yourself:

Do I trust myself to do my job well? Why or why not?

What will I do to ensure I fully trust myself to deliver on my roles and responsibilities?

Do I perform my job consistently at the highest of levels? Why or why not?

What will I do to ensure I am more consistent moving forward?

Do I trust my team members? Why or why not?

Do I trust the leadership team of the organization? Why or why not?

Do my team members, guests, and organization trust me? Why or why not?

How will I continue to earn the trust of my team members, guests, and organization?

Questions to Ask Your Leadership Team:

On a scale of 1 to 10, how well do we trust our team members to deliver extraordinary service?

What will we do to better support them and allow them to do their jobs?

What do we currently do to ensure we have our "aces in their places"—our people in roles where their natural talents and abilities are showcased?

What do we currently do to evaluate the level of trust between our various teams/departments?

What will we do to improve the level of trust between our various teams/departments?

How do we currently measure our consistency of performance?

How will we enhance that measurement to ensure we have continued improvement and forward progress?

On a scale of 1 of 10, what is the level of trust our guests have in us to consistently deliver our brand promise?

What will we do to improve on this level of trust?

On a scale of 1 to 10, what is the level of trust among this leadership team?

What have we done to improve the level of trust on this team?

What have we done to lessen the level of trust on the team?

Questions to Ask Your Staff/Team:

On a scale of 1 to 10, what is your level of trust in your team members to deliver our brand promise?

What are some ideas about how we could better trust our fellow team members and teams?

On a scale of 1 to 10, what is your level of trust in the leadership team of the organization?

What are the ways in which this level of trust in the leadership team could be improved?

On a scale of 1 to 10, what is the level of trust our guests have in us to consistently deliver our brand promise?

What will we do to improve this level of trust?

Do we tend to stay focused on our own jobs and roles? Or do we sometimes get into the habit of focusing on other people—what they are doing, what they should be doing, what they're not doing? How much productivity do we lose to this?

ACTION STEPS

- Be very clear about who you are as a brand. Team members and guests trust brands that are very clear and consistent.

- Inconsistent performance kills a brand, kills relationships. Use the standards you develop in your commitment to Energy x Execution to maintain total commitment to consistency.

- Put your "aces in their places"—have people working to their strengths, doing what they love. By doing so, you create consistency, and consistency leads to trust.

- Be cautious about training new team members with guests. Invest in training and developing them prior to guest engagement.

- Give team members the tools to be successful, and then let them shine!

- Trust yourself to do your job to the best of your ability (Energy x Execution). Trust your team members to do theirs. This creates an "orchestra" that sounds, looks, and feels beautiful—everyone working together, doing their best!

- Stephen M.R. Covey's book, *The Speed of Trust*, teaches that people decide whether or not to trust you based off of two things:

    - Character (Energy)

    - Competence (Execution)

- Focus on developing your team members to continuously say and do things that promote trustworthiness. Tom Peters, leadership speaker and author of *The Pursuit of Wow!*, has always taught that customers stop doing business with you because of:

    - People on your team/Poor relationships (70 percent)

    - Price (15 percent)

    - Product quality (15 percent)

- Become the business culture that creates likability and trust. People do business with people they like and trust. Without trust, you will not have a sustainable business.

- *Earn trust—earn it.* The wise Henry Ford also once said, "You cannot build a reputation on what you say you are going to do." You have to go out and make it happen:

    Decide it. Develop it. Declare it. Deliver it.

- Choose to be a Hospitality from the HEART culture and then begin putting the work in to become it.

Now It's Up to You

Here's the thing about organizations: if you're going to have a group or business, you're going to have a culture. Your culture is being formed and reformed every day, by every person on the team, by every action and moment of inaction. Whether you think about it, talk about it, or act on it, you *will* have a culture. According to leadership guru Peter Drucker, "Culture eats strategy for breakfast." So the only question becomes this: Are you willing to roll the dice and see what happens? Or do you want to be intentional, to be "on purpose" with your organizational culture?

If you've read this far, we hope you already know the answer to that question.

Share this book with the people on your team. Use the quiz in the next section to discover more about your organization's culture. You will be amazed by what you learn! Test the tools and action steps to see which work best for you. Come up with some on your own. Become the type of place where anything is possible. If you, as a leader, believe it, your people will believe it, too. Share your ideas, questions, and stories with us and with the Hospitality from the HEART community. We'd love to hear from you.

Visit: HospitalityFromTheHeart.com

or contact us at:
brandon@HospitalityFromTheHeart.com
katherine@HospitalityFromTheHeart.com

Most importantly, as a leader and in your life, listen to your HEART, as it always speaks the truth.

Hospitality from the HEART Culture
√ Engaged Employees
√ Extraordinary Service
√ Loyal Guests

HOSPITALITY FROM THE HEART QUIZ

Mark each statement that is TRUE for your organization's culture.

❏ Our culture is one where I feel encouraged and confident to share new ideas and ways about how we can better connect and serve our guests.

❏ Our culture is one where I trust my team members to do their jobs to the best of their abilities.

❏ Our culture is one where I have clear expectations of our standards for delivering our service and product.

❏ Our culture is one where I feel we genuinely care for our team members and our guests.

❏ Our culture is one where I have the freedom and authority to make decisions and take action to serve our guests.

❏ Our culture is one where we celebrate and learn from our successes.

❏ Our culture is one where we celebrate and learn from our mistakes and failures.

❏ Our culture is one where connecting with our guests and creating an extraordinary experience is our number one priority.

❏ Our culture is one where we hold each other accountable to our commitments and standards.

❏ Our culture is one where complaints, whining, and excuses are transformed into solutions.

❏ Our culture is one where open communication and feedback is encouraged and welcomed from both guests and team members.

❏ Our culture is one where the leaders are role models of the Hospitality from the HEART culture.

❏ Our culture is one where we set goals, create development plans, and then work every day toward achieving them.

❏ Our culture is one where we evaluate ourselves and our team daily within the Energy x Execution = Results framework in order to grow, learn, and move forward.

❏ Our culture is one where we each take initiative and are not waiting around to be told what to do by our leaders or team members.

❏ Our culture is one where we are present and focused on each and every guest.

❏ Our culture is one where we respect, communicate, and work well together with other areas and departments.

❏ Our culture is one where we focus on *feeling* as much as *thinking* about how we can better connect and serve our guests.

❏ Our culture is one where I trust the leaders of my team and the overall business.

❏ Our culture is one where our team is very flexible and adaptable to ensure we are always doing what is best to connect with and serve our guests.

❏ Our culture is one where I feel recognized for the work I do.

❏ Our culture is one where team members have an opportunity to do what they do best every day.

❏ Our culture is one where we have the tools, materials, and training to do our jobs.

❏ Our culture and our mission make me feel my job is important.

❏ Our culture is one where feedback is taken very seriously and applied to better serve one another and our guests.

Each statement is worth 1 point. Count the number of statements you have marked, add up your points, and use the following breakdown for where you currently stand on the Five Levels of Results:

0–5	Your culture is **AWFUL.**
6–10	Your culture is **TRANSACTIONAL.**
11–17	Your culture is **GOOD 'NUFF.**
18–22	Your culture is **GREAT.**
23–25	Your culture is **EXTRAORDINARY.**

Now you know where you currently stand. Decide where you want to go—what your standards for your culture will be—and then begin the journey. Start the journey and discussion with your team by asking the Four Power Questions:

1. What's working for us?

2. What's not working for us?

3. What have we learned?

4. What will we do differently moving forward?

ABOUT THE AUTHORS

ABOUT BRANDON W. JOHNSON

Brandon W. Johnson, a.k.a. "Positive Energy Guy," was named an Emerging Leader by *Twin Cities Business Magazine* and is a leadership and hospitality expert, speaker, and author. He has developed tens of thousands of leaders through his leadership trainings, workshops, and keynote speeches, and has more than twenty years of experience in operations and leadership in the hospitality industry, non-profits, training organizations, and higher education. He holds a bachelor's degree in hospitality and tourism management and a master's degree in management technology from the University of Wisconsin–Stout. Brandon lives in Woodbury, Minnesota with his wonderful wife Katie, their two high-energy children Emma and Zachary, and their lovable Yorkie, Jazz.

Learn more at **HospitalityFromTheHeart.com** or **BrandonWJohnson.com**.

Facebook: Positive Energy Guy
Twitter: @posenergyguy

About Katherine Foley Roden

Katherine Foley Roden is a respected leader in the hospitality industry and specializes in organizational development, human resource management, and training. Also a talented writer and coach, Katherine draws upon nearly twenty years of experience in casino and resort management. She has worked with and trained thousands of hospitality employees at all organizational levels—from the cleaning crew to the C-suite. Katherine holds a bachelor of arts degree from the University of Massachusetts and a master's degree in organizational leadership from Lewis University. She has worked and lived throughout the United States. She currently resides in beautiful Ridgeley, West Virginia with her husband Roger and her hopelessly uncoachable but beloved dogs, Sasha and Luke.

Learn more at **HospitalityFromTheHeart.com** or
KatherineRoden.com

The Hospitality from the HEART team is dedicated to helping organizations of all kinds lead more from their heart and to function more effectively through better leadership, teamwork, and overall organizational health.

Keynote Speaking: Brandon uses his unique energy, stories, and real-world experience to bring to life the model of HEART to thousands of leaders each year at conferences and organizational events—no event is too big or too small.

Consulting & Workshops: Brandon and Katherine employ the HEART approach in all of their consulting and workshop engagements. With a variety of service offerings —from an overview to full-day workshops—all sessions are practical and highly interactive.

Coaching: Katherine brings the model of HEART to life via individual and group coaching opportunities that ensure the full appreciation, understanding, and consistent application of the HEART principles.

Leadership Trainings: Brandon leads 10—15 of your leaders into an intense and unique 2-day Leadership from the Heart intensive that takes the HEART principles to a whole new level. No PowerPoint. No lecture. No fluff. Just your team learning, growing, and being challenged to live and lead from the heart.

For more tools and information, visit:
HospitalityFromTheHeart.com
or contact us at:
Brandon@HospitalityFromTheHeart.com
Katherine@HospitalityFromTheHeart.com

What is being said about Brandon's two-day Leadership from the Heart training:

"What we got out of these two days is unbelievable and almost immeasurable. This is not taught anywhere. My people already have the technical skills—the best in the upper Midwest. What we didn't have was heart, passion, courage, commitment and respect. We didn't really know each other . . . each other's fears and hopes, dreams, families and loves. This course isn't about teaching, it is about transformation! You will become a better person personally and professionally."

—BILL MORRISSEY, FOUNDER AND CEO OF MORRISSEY HOSPITALITY COMPANIES, ST. PAUL, MN

"The transformational learning process you have integrated into the two-day Leadership from the Heart training is one of the best that I have observed, experienced, or developed in my forty-seven years of leadership and leader development."

—DR. LARRY LINDSAY, CHIEF OF STAFF, INDIANA WESLEYAN UNIVERSITY AND FORMER VP FOR THE ZIG ZIGLAR CORPORATION

For more information about the LFTH Training, visit:
BrandonWJohnson.com *or contact Brandon at*
Brandon@HospitalityFromTheHeart.com